THE BRIDE'S
GUIDE TO FREEBIES

THE BRIDE'S GUIDE TO FREEBIES

Enhancing Your Wedding without Selling Out

BY SHARON NAYLOR

Author of more than thirty-five wedding,
party-planning, and family celebrations books

LYONS PRESS
Guilford, Connecticut

An imprint of Globe Pequot Press

For Joe

To buy books in quantity for corporate use
or incentives, call **(800) 962-0973**
or e-mail **premiums@GlobePequot.com.**

Lyons Press is an imprint of Globe Pequot Press.

Spot art licensed by Shutterstock.com
Text Design: Ann Pawlick
Project Editor: Tracee Williams
Layout: Mary Ballachino

Library of Congress Cataloging-in-Publication Data

Naylor, Sharon.
The bride's guide to freebies : enhancing your wedding without selling out / by Sharon Naylor.
p. cm.
ISBN 978-0-7627-8001-3
1. Weddings—Costs. 2. Free material. 3. Weddings—Planning. I. Title.
HQ745.N385 2013
392.5—dc23

2012011113

Printed in the United States of America

10 9 8 7 6 5 4 3 2 1

Contents

CONTENTS

Acknowledgments

Many thanks to my agents Meredith Hays and Becky Vinter and the entire team at Fine Print Literary Management, including Stephany Evans and Peter Rubie, for helping *me* help *you* with a constant flow of fabulous book deals.

My editor Katie Benoit Cardoso at Globe Pequot is not only a wonderful editor and friend, but she was a beautiful bride! Thanks, Katie, for inviting me into the GPP family.

My husband, Joe, was so worth waiting for! It's a great gift to get to marry someone you like as well as love beyond all comprehension. Some tips in this book come from his groom experience, and I couldn't ask for a better sounding board.

And big hugs to all of the wedding vendors, brides, grooms, parents, and bridal party members who shared their stories and warnings with me, all to help *you* land fabulous freebies to make your wedding dreams come true.

Note from the Author

I've never believed in the old adage *You get what you pay for.* Sometimes you get a whole lot more, including the priceless sentiment when you wear your mother's wedding day necklace or affix your grandmother's saint medallion to your bouquet. The freebies you collect as you plan your wedding may be valuable in and of themselves, but they become ever more valuable as part of the experience you're planning for your Big Day, as well as every celebration around it. Every little piece, like every single crystal in the full effect of your wedding dress, adds up to an amazing, unforgettable result—the day of your dreams.

All throughout this book, I've emphasized respectful asking, and respectful borrowing from anyone who plays a part in your wedding preparations, and I know you'll be one of those wonderful brides who practices good give-and-take. When a vendor throws in a freebie, share the news. Help that vendor survive in his or her field by giving back a precious gift: word-of-mouth referrals and social network spotlighting. Remember, vendors have bills to pay. They have products and supplies to buy, staffs to pay, kids to feed. They're excellent people who liked you enough to throw an add-on your way. It's just good karma to help them in return.

And for the loved ones who freebie you up, it's a Must to send them a handwritten thank-you note with your heartfelt appreciation. When you're inspired to, send a gift as well. It doesn't erase the freebie—it's an entirely different thing: a kindness from you, the loved one they cared enough to help out.

Share your best freebie stories with us on my Facebook page, or tweet me at @sharonnaylorwed, and you can win a little extra freebie. I'm always running contests with my corporate sponsors, and when I see you've given me a shout-out, you'll be entered to win. I don't just advise the give-and-take, I live it. Your stories may also be in future editions of this book.

I wish you all the best as you plan your wedding, and remember to *enjoy* it. The money issue works for you, not the other way around. Take time to breathe in the fun of these wedding tasks, and look at your fiancé every day not just as a co-planner of the wedding, but as the co-planner of your future.

Go and enjoy! I wish you every happiness!

~ Sharon Naylor

Sign Up for the Latest Freebies, Contests, and Giveaways

Just for readers of this book, I'm offering a free weekly newsletter that will lead you right to the greatest freebies, contests, sweepstakes, and giveaways—not to mention awesome apps and fun new resources—that I find for you.

Sign up for my newsletter by e-mailing sharonnaylor freebies@hotmail.com, and I'll put you on the list.

And be sure to follow me at @sharonnaylorwed, where I run my own contests and giveaways each month.

Introduction

Congratulations on your engagement! Your dream wedding is about to become a reality, and you're going to get even more from your wedding budget *because you now hold in your hands the secrets to getting some elements of your big day for free.*

That's right. *Free.*

Even better, you'll find out how to get lots and lots of freebies for all of those parties *around* your wedding day, helping everyone close to you—your parents, your bridesmaids, your friends—save money as well.

Imagine . . . a free $600 wedding tiara. A free $3,000 wedding cake. Free $700 cocktail party stations. Free centerpieces, copies of your wedding video, champagne, an enormous dessert bar, your *wedding shoes.*

All of the secrets are right here in this book: I've provided smart 'Here's What to Say' scripts to help you word your freebie requests perfectly—and be more likely to get them. I've included my favorite freebie and discount resources, and I'll shine a light on what wedding vendors say they're most likely to offer as freebies.

Wedding Experts Included

Yes, you're going to be able to work with wedding vendors. Great ones. Brilliant ones. Ones who are successful enough in their businesses to *give* quality freebies or save you enough money to make *other* items on your wish list free.

No, we're not going to have your Uncle Charlie take your wedding video as a way to save money. **We're not cutting out the wedding vendors.** They're way too important to every aspect of your wedding, including bringing your visions to life with their artistry, revealing creative strategies that work within your budget, *avoiding expensive mistakes,* handling time-consuming tasks, and working their magic to *find you even more freebies along the way.*

Great wedding pros are the *best* resources you have for getting *smart* freebies in every area of your wedding plans. You'll find out here what today's experts are giving away for free and how to be *that bride* whom they *want* to give free things to. That's perhaps the biggest freebie-magnet of all.

And even if you're offered a discount rather than a freebie on an important element of your day, the money you saved can unlock a few hundred dollars in your budget to get something else for free, like a cocktail party station or extra wedding photos. The math all works together, and even the littlest freebies add up.

We're not stopping at little freebies, though. This book can land you a free honeymoon worth $10,000, or $25,000 *cash* to spend on your wedding. Free dresses for all of your bridesmaids or $5,000 in free florals and decor—big-ticket elements that really impress.

Free for Me, Free for You

Freebies very often come in the form of items *lent* or *given to you* by friends and family members. Throughout this book, you'll find lots of ideas on borrows, which are actually a huge freebie for *the giving person.* Here's how it works: When a friend lends you her tiara, you call that her wedding gift to you. She then doesn't have to write a $300 wedding gift check to the two of you, giving her a welcome break to her budget. These win-wins are sprinkled throughout the book as a top trend in finding fantastic freebies within your circle of loved ones. You'll find out what to ask for, how to ask, and how to arrange all the details of a Smart Borrow.

Boxes of Help

As you read through this book, you'll see little boxes with different kinds of tips in them, some to give you the perfectly worded request and some to help you avoid disaster through the *wrong* freebie. They are:

- Disaster! Warns against wedding-wrecking freebie mistakes

- What to Expect: What can happen, good or bad, after you ask a vendor for a freebie, a friend for a borrow

- That's Going to Cost You: Warns about freebies that can cost more in the long run

- Get It in Writing: Important clauses to add to a contract to protect your freebie deal

- Here's What to Say: Actual "how to say it" scripts for making successful freebie requests

- Real Stories: Anecdotes from brides on what they scored for free and from vendors on what they give for free

You're about to start your freebie-hunting mission, together with your groom and everyone else around you. Share these ideas with your parents and bridal party so that *they* can score some freebies as well, and always keep in mind that you're looking for *smart* freebies, not ones that are going to leave you disappointed, ones that look tacky or cheap, ones that *cause* wedding day disasters.

Never be afraid to say no to a freebie offer that doesn't sit right with you.

This is your wedding day and your season of wedding celebrations. Fantastic freebies are only valuable if you love what you get from them and if they help you afford the big, high-priority elements you want, like a designer gown, a great photographer and videographer, your dream wedding cake.

What matters most is not the dollars you saved, but the ultimate dream wedding you saved by being a smart freebie-hunter. Let's get started.

Part One: Freebie-Finding Strategy

We're starting off with the basics that apply to *everyone* you could possibly get a freebie from. You'll learn how to ask, how *not* to ask, and even the quite common situation of not having to ask at all! In today's fiercely competitive wedding industry, more and more bridal vendors are calling it a smart marketing strategy to offer a handful of select freebies right at the outset, winning you, the bride, over and ideally getting you to tell all of your friends how awesome the vendors are.

Pay special attention to chapter 4 on how *not* to ask for freebies—because the fact remains: Wedding experts grant freebies to brides and grooms they *like;* this is what I call the "Like Factor." And you're going to find out exactly how to be liked by them.

CHAPTER 1

Getting the Add-On

Throughout this book, you're going to discover a lot of inside secret scripts on what to say and how to say it when you're asking for an add-on to the service you've booked with a professional or for a borrow or freebie from a friend or relative.

Here we begin with some smart FYIs on how to tap into all of the freebies that wedding experts are ready to offer you. There's a lot of adding-on happening in today's competitive wedding market, and the smartest brides and grooms are cashing in left and right.

What Vendors Are Offering You

Good news first: Vendors often throw in an add-on to your booked package. It's a reality of the wedding industry that brides and grooms who book pricier packages, larger weddings, and grander celebrations might be the recipients of a greater number of freebies, as wedding vendors appreciate the bigger bucks coming to them. But if you're on a lower budget, you're still in the running for these great freebies, too.

Here's that Like Factor again: If you're on a budget and booking the budget packages, many vendors will throw in some freebies to help you out. When they like you, and you have a great rapport, a respectful and friendly demeanor, these professionals show their appreciation for how lovely it is to work with you by adding a few extra elements or upgrades. Why? Because you make their day. Before you walked in the door for your meeting, the wedding vendor might have just gotten off the phone with the world's crankiest, rudest, most aggressive, most insulting bride. The vendor wants to bash her head against the wall. And in you walk, a burst of sunshine, smiles, gratitude, and—vendors say this is the big one—a realistic view of what your budget can accomplish. It's those unrealistic brides who want the million-dollar wedding on a $5,000 budget *who actually help you get freebies.*

It's important to keep in mind that many wedding vendors attend "boost your business seminars" at which their most admired idols in the industry encourage them not to sell themselves short, to charge what they're worth, to value their time and effort. They also learn not to underestimate how much giving a bride a freebie can do for their reputation, and thus their future earnings. We live in a social media world, so if a vendor gives you a freebie, you're going to tweet about it or post your admiration for the vendor on Facebook for all your friends to see. Your ten engaged friends check her out, three book her, and that $200 in upgraded floral centerpieces that you received just got your floral designer three $5,000 orders. It's social media math, and a smart marketing strategy. The trend

Real Stories

VENDORS REWARD THEIR FAVORITES

"I love what I do, but honestly, some of these brides make me hate being in the wedding industry. Who do they think they are, talking down to me like that? And I have dozens of *that* kind of bride. So when I see on my schedule that a bride I *love* is coming in, it renews my faith in my career and makes me smile. So if I can, I'm going to reward her for being one of my favorite brides."—Anne, floral designer

of good-news-freebies is encouraging more vendors to write up packages that look like this example from a wedding coordinator:

> ### THE GOLD PACKAGE
> Weekly meetings up to one month prior to the wedding
> Unlimited cell phone access all throughout the planning
> Vendor selection assistance
> Site selection assistance
> Morning-of organization
> FREE: Invitation design assistance, morning-after breakfast coordination,
>   day-after coordination of rental item returns

And more. When a newly engaged bride scouts potential wedding coordinators, florists, cake bakers, and all manner of other bridal experts, she looks at packages from six to eight professionals, on average. And experienced, accredited wedding vendors know that seeing a handful of *already-there* freebies on the price list thrills a bride and groom who are trudging through endless overwhelmingly high-priced packages. These vendors may just win your business.

So the freebies may already be there for you.

When Do Vendors Offer These Freebies?

This is one of my favorite tips: Many wedding vendors offer a handful of freebies at the outset, *and then they may throw in a few more as your wedding approaches.* The reasons they do this may vary:

- They really like you as a person.

- They really like how you roll with it whenever something goes awry in the plans, such as having to choose a different kind of flower.

- They had a wedding cancellation for the week of your wedding, or the earlier time slot on your wedding day, so they have items they already purchased for that wedding that they can't return. So they give them to you.

- Their staff overordered something, and rather than crowd their storage areas, they give the items to you.

- They can't deliver something you wanted, so they'll make it up to you by upgrading your dessert bar or throwing in a free extra cocktail station.

It's just what they do—a few weeks before the wedding, they throw in the upgraded dessert bar for *every* bride and groom they have, knowing how

Real Stories

VENDORS LIKE TO SHOW OFF TO GUESTS

"If I know that the bride and groom have really planned on a low budget, their flowers are small, their menu is on the smaller side, they had to choose just cake instead of cake and a dessert bar, I'll add in some more impressive elements so that the couple's guests can really see what we do here at our banquet hall. Who knows? Maybe someone on their guest list will be planning a bar mitzvah, bat mitzvah, wedding, or corporate gala. It's great for them to see a more impressive array of my chef's work, rather than not seeing my place in a great light because the slim pickings were so distracting."—Henry, wedding hall manager

wonderfully that gift will be received by planning-weary, cash-strapped couples.

Wedding vendors also throw in extras because they've chosen your wedding as the one that potential wedding clients will look at. As a sales strategy, many sites will tell interested engaged couples to poke their heads in the ballroom at 7 p.m. while the party's going strong—not during the dinner hour when everyone's seated and it would be too obvious for a dozen couples to keep opening the door and looking into the room. The manager usually meets these couples at the door; lets them take a quick peek at the grand wedding going on, the enormous dessert spread, the beautiful decor; and ideally books *their* $50,000 weddings. So your wedding is a sales pitch. It happens all the time, and if you're going to get a few great freebies out of it, I'm sure you won't mind the occasional peek from a beaming newly engaged couple.

One common question that couples ask is this: Will you get more freebies during the off-season (outside of the busy wedding months of May to October)? There's no rule about that. But in the off-season, some sites and vendors may have freebies to throw in because they have to order their supplies according to minimums set by their wholesalers. So they have no choice but to order a larger number of, say, centerpiece vases. They might, then, have extra stock to let you use for free.

Another perk of the off-season wedding is that vendors may have a lot of products in their storerooms from last year's weddings. They want to clear out those silver centerpiece pedestal bowls to make room for the hot new brass ones coming in, so they may find it easier to offer you those $25 silver pedestal bowls for free, rather than take up their valuable storage space or pay to ship the bowls back to the company. I got all of my centerpiece bowls for free for just this reason. They didn't match exactly, but they were all ornate silver pedestal bowls that my guests were excited to take home. Everyone won. So the off-season or change-of-season could net you some excellent freebies.

Here's What to Say

"LET ME TAKE THAT OFF YOUR HANDS"

Wedding vendors may have cases of pretty things in their storage area, but they wouldn't feel comfortable saying to you, *"Hey, want some leftover stuff?"* That would be quite insulting, they fear, a statement on your low budget. So *you* should take the lead. Start with, *"I read in a book that florists often have extra items in their storeroom that they plan to get rid of someday, so if you have anything back there that you'd allow us to use, we'd be very open to seeing it."* Some vendors will jump for joy. You just solved their "when will I have time to organize?" dilemma and made their day. And others will say no, since they may have plans to trade the items with other vendors or place them on Freecycle.com, a popular website where people list free-for-the-taking items that others may want and "shop" for freebies they may need within other site-users' listings. It can't hurt to ask, though, and in fact can often help both of you get a valuable benefit.

If the wedding booked at a site for the time slot before yours—say, the 1 p.m. wedding when your wedding's start time is 8 p.m.—features any elements that you might be able to use, such as the same bandstand, specialty lighting effects, or strung lights in the trees, you may be able to use those things for free. The site's staff wouldn't have to spend time clearing those items away. Ask the site if any of its arranged elements can be left in place for your celebration. You can't, of course, use items the earlier-wedding couple rented or paid for, but if there's anything the *site* will create for them, you may be able to get those things at no extra charge, just by asking.

You might also ask the site to provide you with the name of the band the earlier wedding has booked, or their photographer and videographer. If the site agrees to give you their contact information, and if they check out as being the perfect professionals for your day, you can tell them that you're the second wedding at the location they're already going to be at. So could they eliminate their travel and set-up fees for you? By virtue of already being there, they're spending less time on your wedding, so that could add up to a freebie or an add-on in trade.

What You Can Offer Your Vendors

Vendors know you're going to talk with all of your friends and relatives about your wedding plans, and that you're probably well plugged into a big social network. They *know* that you're going to tell your engaged friends about the fabulous wedding coordinator you're working with, or the ultra-talented invitation designer, or the dreamy cake you just tasted.

What to Expect

A LITTLE GIVE AND TAKE

If the couple whose afternoon wedding is before yours is paying for the band to be there, to set up and perform, then *you* should give *them* a freebie by paying for any takedown or cleanup the band requires. You've still gotten a fair amount for free and you're keeping your good karma by not allowing the other couple to pay for the band's takedown as well. For any shared arrangement, you need to have these details written in your contract, as should the other couple.

Tread lightly in trying to use this as a bargaining chip, though. Proclaiming *"If you give us this for free, we'll tell all 800 of our Facebook friends!"* isn't going to carry the weight you think it does. And you could very well offend the wedding expert with such an offer. Their products and time cost them, so when you claim that exposure to your particular circle is worth an equal amount, you look terribly naïve, and you're also devaluing what the expert is putting into your day.

It's okay to mention that you have a lot of engaged friends. They'll catch the potential of your referrals. But stop short of trying to *trade* for it. We'll get more into this in chapter 4 on "How Not to Ask for Freebies," but I mention it here so that you don't make any mistakes before getting to that section.

One incentive you can mention that does carry some weight is if you're submitting your wedding for a Real Weddings feature in a local bridal magazine. *That* gets wedding experts excited, since being featured in even a small bridal magazine shows off their work to five thousand, ten thousand, fifty thousand, or more *local* brides who could potentially book them. And if you're submitting to a bigger national magazine with a three million (or more) circulation, that too serves the wedding experts well by giving them a spectacular credit for their own blogging, Facebooking, or tweeting.

What about blogs covering your wedding? That works, too. Many blogs invite brides-to-be to report for them, to share each step of their planning *now*, showing brides in meetings with their chosen vendors, and sharing the vendors' URLs. Vendors know which big blogs have large audiences, and they also know that major bridal magazines feature real bride bloggers. So if you've landed a blogging gig, share that information with all of your vendors. Don't be shy. Those vendors might just decide they like you even more and may throw in some freebies.

Tell your vendors during a particularly great meeting, or after the expert has delivered a wonderful solution, that you're going to tweet about that or post a glowing review about them on Yelp or WeddingMapper.com

What to Expect

"OUR WEDDING WILL BE IN A MAGAZINE"

If you share the news that your wedding has been chosen for magazine coverage, you're going to have to *prove* it to your vendors before they'll consider granting you a freebie or two. Wedding experts are savvy to a particular con that other couples have pulled—saying their wedding is going to get media coverage as a ploy to get freebies, but then the wedding never appears anywhere. So bring along a copy of your e-mail from the magazine editor requesting images or expressing interest in your event. When you go armed with proof, your wedding experts will have an even greater incentive to create a gorgeous wedding on your budget, one that shows off their talents, which might just motivate them to throw in some freebies along the way.

(a free site where you register to share details about your vendors so that other local couples can ask you about their services). And when you do, send the links to the vendors.

Another way to foster a great, reciprocal relationship with your vendors out of the kindness of your heart, and not just to get freebies, is to tell them you'll send photos of their work from your wedding day that they may be able to use on their websites. Remember, though, that your professional photographer usually owns the rights to the photos he or she takes, so you would have to get permission from your photographer first. They most often say yes, provided they get a photo credit with a link. It's excellent business strategy for them as well. And if you get fabulous photos that friends have taken with their digital cameras, ask their permission to send those photos to your experts for posting on their sites, with the photos credited to your friends. Never send a friend's photo without permission.

And lastly, ask your vendors what you can do for them. If they have a photo shoot planned to upgrade their website, or for their blog, would they like you to be their free model for the afternoon? A few hours spent helping with their professional goals could lead to extra benefits later on.

The "Like" Factor

Being sweet and polite is not the only part of 'The "Like" Factor' that wedding experts say puts a bride and groom on their most favored list. Dozens of experts chimed in about what they love to experience with a wedding couple, and here's what they said:

- Those who send thank-you e-mails when they deliver information or solutions.

- Those who know what they want and stick to it, not flip-floppers who change their mind every day.

- Those who show up for appointments on time, and never pull a no-show. If you have to cancel, do so a few days ahead of time.

- Those who call for important things only, not with every whim.

- Those who honor the vendor's expertise, not questioning every plan or telling her how to do her job.

- Those who do research on their own, Googling easy-to-find answers, not those who act as if the vendor is their personal secretary. "Which kinds of flowers did Kate Middleton have?" is easy for you to find, and a disrespectful waste of your vendor's time.

Disaster!

KEY YOUR BOSSYPANTS PEOPLE AWAY!

Vendors like brides who have pleasant people in their planning circle. This one can be tough if you have a bossy mom or a drama queen mother-in-law. And vendors are quite honest in saying that even if they like the bride, a mom or a maid of honor who's a pill can wreck the goodwill they feel toward the bride. So if you have a troublemaker on your hands, especially a domineering person who acts disrespectfully toward your vendor, perhaps it's best to leave this person out of the meetings. Vendors can handle all personality types, and can defuse a true drama queen, but the extra work saps their energy levels and reflects badly on you.

All of these tips are just the foundation for finding and getting great freebies for your wedding, for your additional wedding season celebrations, and for your honeymoon. Throughout this book, you'll find countless more to build upon, and to maximize with the strength of the lessons you just learned here.

CHAPTER 2

What's Realistic to Ask For

You'll have far more success in securing freebies if you stick to realistic requests. Wedding experts have to buy everything that's needed for your wedding, and the time they spend pre-, during-, and post-wedding to fulfill your wishes is valuable. So asking for $10,000 in free catering isn't going to be well-received. Just the same, asking the videographer to edit your video for free will make him laugh, as the process of video editing is extremely time-consuming, often taking at least triple the time he spent shooting the wedding itself. That's how you get a seamless, gorgeous wedding video, and quality costs money.

To keep from insulting your vendors, or from looking as though you're completely naïve about how much food, liquor, flowers, fabrics, and other items cost, stick with these overall wedding-wide rules to improve your odds of getting a yes when you ask for a freebie:

- Ask what a vendor already has. As mentioned, vendors often have storerooms full of pretty glass vases, pedestal centerpiece bowls, candelabras, linens, and other items left over from prior weddings—or not used because prior weddings were canceled. When you show you're open to this stock, you may get it for free, or at a reduced rate.

- Ask for low-time items. For your cake, dress design, and other detailed elements, it's the labor, those endless hours of handcrafting

What's Not Realistic to Ask For

- Food, flowers, and other large-volume supplies that are expensive for vendors to buy, even at wholesale prices.
- Free labor by vendors' assistants, bartenders, or valets. It's actually illegal to ask for no-pay labor.
- Free shipping or delivery. Fuel is expensive, as is the pay for delivery workers and setup crews, so don't ask for this to be thrown in. (If it's offered to you, however, great!)
- A greater-value item than the one you're replacing. If the florist calls to say peonies aren't available, don't expect pricier orchids as the replacement.
- Extra work from the vendor. This is important. When you book a coordinator, he or she gauges the scope of your wedding, how much work will go into your plans, and how many other weddings he or she can book for that same time. If you start expanding your plans and being the Headache Client, you're not likely to get freebies.

sugar-paste roses on a cake or sewing crystals onto a gown, that elevates cost. When you choose a simpler design element that doesn't take a team hours to make, you may get a portion for free. *"I had a bride who asked for thirty short-cut ranunculus centerpieces, and since they take a few seconds to make, I threw in half for free,"* says one grateful-for-the-easy-task floral designer.

- Limit your freebie-asking to one thing, such as an extra cocktail party station or an extra dessert (like a tray of pretty fruit tarts), not an entire class of free things like an entire $1,000 dessert bar. Managers are far more likely to grant a modest, low-budget request.

- Be open to nonidentical items. A vendor may have small collections of coordinating chargers or table runners to mix and match in your freebie reception decor.

- Ask for what's in-season and plentiful. If your caterer can get bushels of seasonal apples from a local farm for next to nothing, she may throw in extra desserts or a hot cider bar. Visit LocalHarvest.org to see what's in-season in your area during the time of your wedding.

- Ask for a style upgrade. I spoke with Marni Gold from Creative CustomCardBoxes.com about her decorative card boxes that guests pop those gift envelopes into. She said that when a bride orders a two-layer box, she happily adds on an extra decorated layer to make a great impression.

CHAPTER 3

How to Ask for Freebies

Throughout this book, you'll find special 'Here's What to Say' features to help you word your requests diplomatically, with a greater chance of earning a freebie from your wedding experts. These will come in handy as you start to inquire about freebies. Here, first, are some general tips to keep in mind before you ask:

- Make a great first impression, being genuinely happy to work with your expert and enthusiastic about the planning process. Wedding vendors reward their nicest clients with freebies, and they'll shut right down if you ask, *"What's for free?"* right out of the gate. You don't want your vendor's first impression of you to be greedy and disrespectful.

- Convey what's most important to you right at the outset, so that the vendor knows where he or she can help you get more for your money in your top-priority areas.

- Admit that you're on a budget. These days, who isn't? It's quite smart to say, *"We'd love to get any budget-stretchers possible, and we know you'll help us do it in style."*

- Ask directly, with this wording: *"Would it be possible to get (insert item) added on for free?"* which is respectful and defers to the vendor's expertise. In many cases, it *is* possible.

- Ask in person, not through an e-mail. Your friendly in-person presence—and, vendors say, courage—in asking face-to-face often earns a better response than an e-mail, which vendors say can come off as bossy without body language and voice intonations.

- Say thank you no matter what the response. You've asked politely, and it's good etiquette to show gratitude for a request granted *or* considered. If the vendor says yes, send a handwritten thank-you note expressing your happiness over his or her generosity. Vendors love proper brides and will peg you as someone they'd love to help again, if possible.

With the top general tips in mind, read on to discover how to fine-tune your requests, to potentially earn even more freebies than you originally expected.

CHAPTER 4

How Not to Ask for Freebies

Wedding vendors have heard it all. I'm sure many of them have had as much experience with the human psyche and mild psychological disorders as the average psychotherapist. They have something that a person wants, and they've seen everything from sugar-sweet charm to downright blackmail in an effort to get that something for free. And considering that the average wedding vendor is dealing with dozens and dozens of brides, grooms, moms, and 'maids at a time, that's a lot of noise in their brains.

It's just human nature. When someone treats you with respect and consideration, you're motivated to do more for that person. And just the opposite is true; when someone talks down to you, or acts manipulative, you're not going out of your way to do *that person* any favors.

Of course you won't be manipulative, but a tightly wound wedding vendor who's dealing with a ton of Bridezillas can take one little benign comment, classify *you* as a Bridezilla, and place you on the "no extra help" list. And yes, many wedding vendors do have actual lists of difficult brides they vow not to assist beyond the basics in the contract—and they chat with other wedding vendors about those difficult brides. It can be a lot like junior high.

So it's my intention to keep you off the "no extra help" list and off the grapevine by helping you avoid the most common mistakes and misworded requests for wedding freebies.

The Top 10 Ways Not to Ask for a Freebie

Believe it or not, some brides can be stunningly nervy. I've included these jaw-dropping no-no's because, contrary to the large volume of posts on wedding message boards telling brides how awesome it was to muscle her vendor into giving her a freebie, we don't entertain bullies here. So read on to embed a good reminder of what not to say in your requests, and share these tips with any maid of honor, bridesmaid, parent, or friend who's volunteered to help with your wedding plans. Even they need to steer clear of tactics that are just over the line of good manners . . . even if these tactics work like a charm in their shark-tank work world.

1. *Don't offer them a trade for advertising.* Not too long ago, there was a brief blip in wedding world, in which experts were asked to provide their services for free, in exchange for getting an ad in the wedding program or signage at the reception. This isn't a high school football game, with you offering a little square ad in your game-day program. Today's quality professionals will take high offense if you offer them the "chance" to work for free. Pros and novices alike rack up big expenses in acquiring your wedding supplies, paying staff, investing their time, traveling, and more. Asking them to work for no money is the No. 1 wrong thing to do. Would you go to the dentist for a filling and say, "Instead of my paying you, how about

Real Stories

"It doesn't matter what industry a bride works in; I know there are aggressive, pushy, steamroller types in every line of work. But when one tries to use her boardroom barracuda act on me, I'm not giving her a *single* discount, let alone a freebie."—Abbie, floral designer

I tell a few hundred of my friends about you? Maybe half will come to you for dental work?" That's not going to fly. So don't even offer that as a way to get freebies—unless *the vendor* asks for it.

2. *Don't offer to brag about them on social media as a form of currency.* First, that's unethical. And in some cases, illegal. Such offers don't impress wedding vendors, because they know that only a percentage of your Facebook friends are local, and a smaller percentage of those are planning weddings. Besides, quality wedding vendors do their jobs so well, for money, that they know their happy clients will brag about them on Facebook anyway, so this is an empty offer that could get you labeled as a "manipulator."

3. *Dangling the competition.* While you're interviewing six or seven potential floral designers, cake bakers, or entertainers, don't try to play your pro against his or her competition, mentioning the big, valuable freebie another vendor offered. This doesn't deliver the results you expect. All the vendor in front of you is likely to think is that his freebie-slinging competitor must be desperate. You've just reinforced this vendor's superiority, which reminds him he doesn't have to give out big freebies to win business out of desperation, like that pathetic competitor out there.

4. *Dropping names of others who got freebies. "Five years ago, you did my cousin's wedding, and she told everyone how great you were— especially throwing in her entire dessert buffet for free!"* Well, that was five years ago, and this vendor probably doesn't remember your cousin. Plus, the vendor might sniff this story out as a fake. You'd be surprised at what truly heinous brides and grooms with no morals will say to try to get a freebie. They're rare beasts, but wedding vendors can spot them.

5. *Don't ask at the last minute.* The contract is already signed, the terms spelled out, orders placed and paid for by your wedding

vendor—and now you approach your pro with a request for some of your order to be free? That's not going to happen. Vendors have specific language in their contracts spelling out that prices are final, to protect them against these kinds of eleventh-hour requests, and in most cases you'll hear a no. A kindhearted vendor will empathize with you as you shed tears and talk about how angry your fiancé is over the cost of the wedding, but you're not likely to get half your wedding for free because you didn't plan wisely.

6. *Don't ride the sob story.* If you're truly having a disaster, such as a parent pulling out of paying for the wedding after promising to do so, I send you hugs and comfort. That's a terrible position to be in. But you have to tread lightly when it comes to taking your tale of difficulty to your wedding vendor, because even with the greatest of working relationships, you're not always going to get a sympathy freebie. In fact, a businesslike vendor might flag you as a risk for nonpayment and look at you with suspicion. Of course, a vendor who truly likes you may give some friendly assistance. The vendor may offer some of your original plans for less (with the vendor taking a lower profit margin on the order) or suggest that you come in and rework your plans to still get a gorgeous wedding within your new budget. Most vendors are great like that. But savvy vendors are not always going to cave to your sad story and tears—because, again, they may be suspicious of those with tales of woe, and they simply can't survive in business if they chopped in half the bill of everyone with a problem.

7. *Don't use what you are spending with the vendor as leverage.* If you're spending a good deal of money with a vendor, it's never classy to wave that dollar figure around as a manipulation. The vendor is aware of what you're spending on the package and plans you've booked. You were charged for what you asked for. And it's a fast

path to the "don't help" list—not just with this vendor but with all of the ones you've hired.

8. *Don't send in your aggressive friend to "do the deal" for you.* Again, that steamroller friend could get you on the "do not help" list if she's too forceful with her requests. Act on your own behalf, and vendors may like you enough to do more for you. Another element of the aggressive friend being sent in with an aim to "steal" freebies is the *aggressive* parent who's that type—one to bully a kindly pro, then strut out of there like the winner of a title fight. A parent like that gets everyone on the "do not help" list.

9. *Don't quote wholesale prices to the pro.* Would you like it if someone walked into your office and threw down a printout of all the ways they did your job better than you? You can talk wholesale sources at the beginning of your planning with your vendor, such as with

Real Stories

SOME VENDORS GRANT FREEBIES AT THE LAST MINUTE

"I save our freebies until the week before the wedding. If the bride and groom have been nice and respectful during the planning time, I'll thank them for being great to work with by throwing in that extra cocktail party station they wanted, or by bumping them up to a higher bar package. They haven't asked. I just like them and want to do something special for them. And in the hectic weeks before the wedding, that makes them *so* happy they can't even express it."—Bill, catering manager

a wedding coordinator getting you a great collection of favors for your reception, but when the date draws near, you can't pick through completed tasks and say, *"I found these for $1.49 each at (company), so surely you can throw my favors in as a freebie."* Vendors aren't going to want to reward you for doing detective work behind their backs and then expecting a price drop because you told them so. Those vendors would more likely have fantasies of tripling the price on you.

10. *Don't e-mail or text the request.* Speaking directly to the vendor, preferably in person, is the best way to show your visible signs of gratitude and assess his or her receptiveness. None of that comes through in an e-mail, and some vendors say they wonder if a basic "Hey, we're running low on cash—any chance you can throw us a little freebie?" e-mail was sent to *all* of the wedding vendors.

11. *Don't kiss butt.* My wedding vendor friends asked me to add in this extra one. It's so easy to Google any professional to find out the wedding television shows she's been on, the bridal industry awards she's been nominated for or won, the celebrity wedding expert who partnered with her on a big event, and more. Wedding pros don't mind that you admire their accomplishments, but they worked hard for them. They spent days working on a two-hundred-page entry for that award. It's something they're greatly proud of, and as nice as it is to hear you list their high-profile accomplishments and awards, it's quite transparent. *"You're kissing my butt to get me to give you something,"* a wedding vendor insider says. *"And that's not going to work on me."*

These tips will help you work smoothly with your vendors, and when you show your bridesmaids and parents this list, they too can forge quality relationships with the vendors they choose for the parties they'll plan, perhaps earning them freebies and budget-breaks as well.

Part Two:

Freebies from Wedding Vendors

And now . . . it's time.

Now that you know the basic dos and don'ts, it is time to take notes, flag pages, and get ready to fine-tune your freebie-hunting strategies. First, a universal tip that can get you freebie after freebie—why not start with one of the smartest and most effective money-saving strategies out there? We're talking *gift cards*.

Many wedding vendors offer gift cards for their services, and if you don't see them offered on their site, ask for them. I've spoken to hundreds of wedding vendors who say they would *create* a wedding gift certificate or card if a bride and groom wanted to tell their families to get them gift cards for their services for their birthday or holiday gifts.

While some vendors recommend adding a note to your personal wedding website, saying that your vendors offer gift cards, *"so please help us out!,"* I feel better about advising you to avoid a potential etiquette offense and simply tell parents, siblings, and best friends that this is what you'd like for personal gifts over the next year. Etiquette sensitivity is more relaxed with your closest loved ones, and their gifts can add up to hundreds of dollars in freebies from your vendors. This section will also share a great big warning about winning wedding vendor freebies, such as those big-ticket prizes you often find at bridal shows and on wedding blogs. Without fail, always check out the wedding vendor and his or her company to be sure they're accredited and experienced before you hand them your Big Day. You don't want your big freebie win to turn out to be a nightmare.

CHAPTER 5

Wedding Coordinator

Wedding coordinators are quite outspoken about their displeasure with brides and grooms asking for severely slashed prices or for unwise freebies. A noted wedding coordinator recently spoke to a major conference of wedding planners and vendors, practically on fire with anger over couples trying to take advantage of her. *"I deliver nothing until I get paid,"* she said. *"I'm in business to sell, and to sell business for my vendors!"* Hundreds in her audience retweeted her battle cry of "charging your proper value."

According to TheWeddingReport.com, the national average spent on wedding coordinator services is $1,270. In some regions, that's an extremely low figure, and if you require a wedding coordinator to travel to a destination wedding spot with you, that would probably only cover her travel expenses.

Why are many professional wedding coordinators so averse to handing out freebies? Because they provide immensely valuable services, and they spend a *lot* more time on your wedding details than you see. They're working their networks, going through databases, walking you step-by-step through the process using their expensive computer software and templates. They have staff members, office expenses that are higher now than ever before, and sky-high insurance fees, and they have to purchase all of those linens and centerpiece bowls and decor items you put on your list. Plus, they work weekends.

So rather than risk angering the person who holds your wedding in his or her hands by asking for a freebie beyond the already-free initial consultation meeting, look instead at the *priceless* things that you enjoy within the planner's wedding package:

Items Worth More Than Free

- Connections to top-quality vendors who will work according to your budget and—the planner knows—may be amenable to giving a freebie or two. (Right here, the coordinator is a strong part of your freebie-finding strategy, being your conduit to those who *do* give freebies.)

- Knowledge of unique locales that work in your budget, such as estate homes or museums.

- Contract review expertise. A great planner is an expert at contract terms and can spot extra charges in the small print, negotiating them out for you.

- Keeping you organized. With free, upgraded planning worksheets, spreadsheets, and the use of the coordinator's high-tech software, your plans and budget stay on track, and you stay stress-free . . . which keeps you from overspending.

- Conflict resolution with the moms, or with fussy bridesmaids or difficult vendors, using his or her mastery in mediation and diplomacy to prevent changes to your plans, wasted money, extra charges, and headaches.

- Overseeing everything on the wedding day, so that you can enjoy your salon visit and prewedding photos prewedding. Neither you nor your family has to deal with overseeing deliveries, setup, decorating, and tracking down missing items. An organized and efficient pro is on the case.

> ## Real Stories
>
> ### WEDDING COORDINATORS
> ### PREVENT DOUBLE PAYMENTS
>
> "We know the best suppliers who offer quality products, the ones that get the order right the first time so that you don't have to waste money on replacement items."
> —Dena, wedding coordinator

- Running the last-minute switch to Plan B for an outdoor wedding, such as relocating the wedding to an indoor spot.

- Helping with destination wedding legalities, such as obtaining a marriage license overseas.

What They Do Offer for Free

Quality professionals do know that you would be thrilled with a little freebie or two. It's just good business, winning your admiration and perhaps referrals to other weddings in your circle of friends. So they may give out—for free—a wedding binder, wedding planning and ideas books, bridal magazines, a free personal wedding website (with countdown clocks and video stream) that they have a clients-only code for, a wedding garter or unity candle, guest books, and other low-cost items that can save you anywhere from $10 to $100 or more.

Besides the money-saving brilliance of your own wedding coordinator, and all of the perks you get from that partnership, don't forget that you have free access to priceless wedding ideas, images, tips, top ten lists, and inside scoop from the world's top wedding coordinators on their blogs,

Real Stories

REFERRALS TO YOUR COORDINATOR
CAN GET YOU FREEBIE-MONEY

"I offer a referral program. If a bride and groom refer me to their friends, and their friends book me for their weddings, I'll take $200 to $300 off of the original bride and groom's tab in thanks for the new clients."—Jeannie, wedding coordinator

Expert tip: Some wedding coordinators limit the number of referral discounts they'll grant to one couple. They still do have to purchase all of your wedding supplies, so most often, you can't zero out your tab by referring thirty wedding couples. Still, a break of $600 to $900 will fund a nice collection of freebies in other areas of your wedding plans.

websites, Facebook pages, Twitter feeds, and in special interviews on the top bridal sites.

You might not be able to book Colin Cowie or Preston Bailey for your wedding plans, but your wedding can get a little touch of Colin's and Preston's amazing inspirations for *free*. Look out for Twitter chats with your favorite wedding pros, listen to Martha Stewart Weddings satellite radio for free wedding tips from Martha and her top experts, and pay attention to tweeted quotes from celebrity wedding coordinators' live appearances, where top-name pros share their best budget-planning secrets and design inspirations. *The wedding bloggers tweeting these quotes paid $600 or so to attend this celeb-studded event, and you get the best gems from the event for free.*

CHAPTER 6

Ceremony

Where you have your ceremony could make all the difference in your budget. Different locations offer different freebie opportunities, and while it's true that having an outdoor, beach, or backyard wedding would require you to spend a lot on rentals (chairs, a trellis, etc.), it's not an automatic rule that this kind of setting is always going to cost you more, as you may have read online.

First, to lay the groundwork, let's look at some stats from TheWeddingReport.com's 2011 study:

- Couples holding both their ceremony and reception at the *same location:* 55.8 percent

- Couples holding their ceremony at one place and their reception at another location: 44.2 percent

- For those same-location weddings, 63.3 percent are outdoor, and 36.7 percent are indoor.

- For same location weddings, officiant cost is $232, and ceremony accessories are $182.

- For different locales, 78.2 percent are indoor, and 21.8 percent are outdoor.

- Since having different locations most often means the ceremony is held at a house of worship, with the reception elsewhere, the survey's report of 72.5 percent of these taking place in a church or religious location makes sense. Another 7.5 percent are in gardens or parks, and other locations include beaches (4.9 percent) and wedding chapels (4.3 percent).

- For different location weddings, ceremony location costs $778, the officiant costs $253, and ceremony accessories cost $184.

What You Can Get for Free

For both types of ceremony locations, the prices are hefty, and it makes sense, since the ceremony is the most important element of the day. But there are some location-specific freebies you may be able to arrange.

Get It In Writing

SURVEY AVERAGES JUST GIVE YOU BALLPARK FIGURES, NOT IRONCLAD AMOUNTS

Always demand that the actual price of a wedding item or service be written into your contract, not any vague price range, such as $150 to $250, that a vendor has looked up in a wedding industry survey. It's great for you to know what couples near you are spending, on average, at CostOfWedding.com, but those numbers are never contract-worthy specifics. If specific amounts can't be quoted now, don't sign the contract now.

AT A HOUSE OF WORSHIP

One top benefit of houses of worship is that they regularly host weddings and as such often have a large supply of items they may be willing to let you use for free. Many brides and grooms, as well as some houses of worship, have reported that membership in the house of worship—such as your being a parishioner—is often required for the church or synagogue to take on your wedding. After all, they want to save their available Saturdays for members of their congregation. Houses of worship may reward your or your family's long-standing membership and volunteer works with greater access to their wedding supplies and decor items.

Now, this is not to say that all churches will turn you down if you're not a regular church-goer or that you have to be on ten volunteer boards to get free candles. Just be aware that being a member could have its privileges, making it easier for you to ask for freebies. But ask anyway. The nature of a house of worship is to welcome all into its community, and the best-run worship centers are very willing to embrace you, your wedding, and your requests.

What can you often get for free? Here's a list of the most common items:

- Candle stands on the rows or pews, as well as fresh, white candles from their bulk supplies.

- A standard, white, non-slip aisle runner.

- An altar or a standard chuppah.

- An already floral-filled location, if the house of worship keeps its setting filled with fresh, potted flowers, lilies, carnations, and at Christmastime, a sea of poinsettias. (Tip: Ask about the site's already-planned florals and decor when you discuss your wedding date with the officiant.)

Here's What to Say

A FREE PERFORMANCE
THAT ALSO DOES A BIT OF GOOD

When approaching houses of worship about ceremonial music, consider this request wording:

You: "Would the children's choir be available to sing during our ceremony?"

Officiant: "They do practice on Saturday mornings, and we usually charge $150 to have any of our choirs perform for weddings, funerals, or special services."

You: "We're on a tight budget and can't do the $150, but I thought I'd ask if you and the chorus director would consider our wedding as an opportunity for the children to practice performing in front of an audience, just for one song."

Officiant: "For one song? Yes, I think we can make that happen for you."

Now if you have some money in your wedding budget, it's a nice gesture to give the choir a donation of $50 or whatever you can manage, with your thanks.

- Existing beautiful lighting effects, courtesy of specialty lighting or the glow from the midday sun through stained glass windows.

- Air conditioning and heating (which may sound like nothing, but consider the high cost of renting these comfort machines for an outdoor wedding!).

- Use of the site's indoor setting and outdoor grounds for your wedding photos, which is a big savings over what other couples pay for permits to take photos in state parks and arboretums.

- The availability of ceremony music, such as an organists' or pianists' performance offered as part of the ceremony fee, or for a modest fee, a performance by the church's youth or adult choir. Use of the house of worship's sound system for any musician or singer you hire or arrange to perform during your ceremony.

Don't forget that adult choirs may have an extra-special event coming up, such as performing for a visiting cardinal. Your offer to be their practice audience also applies, if you inquire.

FREEBIES FROM OTHERS

Don't forget that you can borrow items for your ceremony locale from recently wed friends and family, or borrow ceremony items from others

That's Going to Cost You

ALWAYS CHECK FIRST

Before you arrange for anyone to make decor items, or to borrow friends' ceremony decorations, always check with the house of worship to see if it allows outside decor items to be brought in. Some sites have strict rules about what they will and won't allow for ceremony decorations, either because of their concerns about damage to their marble or hardwood floor from a nonstick aisle runner or simply because their value system calls for modestly-decorated wedding ceremonies to keep the focus on the vows and service.

in your circle of loved ones. A friend whose wedding took place just a few months ago may be willing to lend you the unmonogrammed lavender aisle runner she bought for her big day or let you use her chuppah that her uncle made for her and that you can decorate with flowers and crystals.

Since the ceremony may include religious, spiritual, or cultural elements like a gold cup from which the bride and groom sip wine, you may borrow your parents' wedding-day chalice. Or your sister's braided cord from her cultural handfasting ritual, or baskets your best friend used for her flower girl's petals, or even the ring pillow your cousin used at her wedding, just with a fresh ribbon tie that matches your wedding colors.

Your unity candle may be a meaningful gift from your grandparents, or a DIY-talented friend can make your unity candle as her wedding gift to you.

And special, beaded tablecloths owned by your mother-in-law can be used as the altar decor.

AT AN ALTERNATIVE LOCATION

Alternative locations will most often require you to rent a great many items, and they likely don't have a stockpile of candles the way a house of worship would. But it is wise to ask what you may be allowed to use in your ceremony decor. The site manager may take you on a fabulous tour of the grounds lit up by existing lighting systems, with bubbling fountains, ponds, and marble terraces surrounded by blooming floral gardens and plantings.

It's the scenery that becomes your greatest freebie at unique locations, indoors or out. Amazing architecture, grand gardens, spectacular views of the ocean or the city skyline—they all create a magical wedding location and may even preclude you from having to pay for any other florals or decor. The natural beauty of the site can add up to an entirely free decor budget. Yes, the location may cost a few hundred to book, but in most cases, so does the house of worship. Many of those charge wedding fees, officiant fees, and even fees for the caretaker to prepare and clean

Get It In Writing

DON'T BOOK A TENT WITHOUT ASKING FIRST

Always check with sites for permission to put up a tent on their grounds. Some sites forbid the structure, since they don't want their lawn ruined by dozens of stakes or flattened by flooring tiles. Before you put down a deposit on any tenting or outdoor party space supplies, always get permission *in writing* first, so that you don't waste several hundred dollars of nonrefundable money if you find out later that's a Don't for them.

the church or synagogue before and after your ceremony. So look at this freebie decor offering as an entirely separate entity. It could save you more than $3,000 in ceremony decor flowers.

If your location is outdoors and requires a tent, which is smart to use even on an expected comfortable day, your tent rental cost may be covered in this huge savings, making it mathematically free.

The same borrowable items discussed earlier, such as aisle runners, ceremony cups, and ring pillows, apply to this ceremony location, too, and you might also borrow a friend's quality speaker system so that your guests can hear you recite your vows. An outdoor location is often breezy, which can carry your words away.

Free Officiant

At many non-house-of-worship weddings, brides and grooms find their own officiants, and one option is to have a friend perform the ceremony. He or she might get ordained through an accredited online service for under $50, which might be counted as his or her wedding gift to you, if offered. It *is* considered proper etiquette for you to offer to pay for the ordination fee, if this person is getting ordained only for you.

Keep in mind that there may be complicated rules to having a friend ordained for the ceremony. Read the fine print carefully, and speak to a representative at your wedding location's town hall, to confirm your friend as a recognized officiant, meeting all requirements.

Still, even with the fee and the extra research time, it's a big savings over the $232 to $253 officiant fees you read about earlier.

Additional Ceremony Freebies

Since the ceremony is the centerpiece of your wedding day, fill it with special wording, sounds, and sentimental touches. These may all be free:

- Find sample wedding vows for free online.

- Look at free quotation sites like QuoteGarden.com and on Twitter (@TheLoveStories) to find appropriate quotations to use in your wedding ceremony and your wedding programs.

- Go to the library to find beautiful poetry and quotation books for your ceremony words.

- If a friend will perform at the ceremony as his or her gift to you, find free sheet music online for him or her to learn.

- Research cultural and spiritual ceremony rituals online.

- Skip the cost of post-ceremony bubbles or birdseed and just allow guests to applaud your new union.

CHAPTER 7

Invitations and Print Items

Whatever you do, don't skip print invitations. Many brides seeking freebies or keeping within a tight budget ask if it's okay to send Evites to the wedding. That's an Etiquette Don't. Plus, you'd regret later not having pretty, textured, tangible invitations to frame, and your guests wouldn't think too highly of an e-mailed invitation, even if you say it's for eco-friendly reasons.

Save the Evites for the rehearsal dinner, after-party, and wedding morning breakfast. Those are some fantastic freebies and perfectly fine for those events.

What about DIY invitations? Given the cost of paper stock and the high cost of printer ink, making your own invitations and print items isn't anywhere near a freebie. I wish I had better news for you in this section, but paper, ink, and embellishments do cost money no matter where you get them.

The freebies are here, though. Here's what you might get. . . .

Invitations

When you order professionally made invitations from a designer or an online site, paper supplies and design time cost money, but you might be offered a "twenty-five invitations free" incentive. Or free inner envelopes. Or free shipping.

That's Going to Cost You

DON'T DELAY YOUR ORDER WHILE HOPING TO WIN YOUR PRINT ITEMS

Of course, you might win your invitations or Save-the-Dates at a bridal show or through a wedding site or blog, which would be fantastic news. But don't hold off on your order, waiting to see if you win yet another contest. If you delay too long, you'll have to pay expensive rush fees to get your Save-the-Dates or invitations on time.

Some companies will give you a free upgrade to their premium tier of font styles, and some won't charge for a second ink color. Some will give you the outer envelopes for free, and some will throw in patterned or colored envelope liners, as well as free response cards. So some *elements* of your invitations package might be yours *gratis*. Each company, each designer maintains its own policies about add-ons for paying customers. You have to search around and ask what's free in each package.

When parents look for a portion of the wedding to pay for, this is a category that they often choose. You will, of course, select the design and create your wording, but the invitations suite—as it's called in the industry—is their gift to you. Which makes it a very lovely freebie.

Additional Print Items on the House

It would be rare to find a reception hall that doesn't provide table number cards, so check to see that it's a freebie you can count on, and ask if your site provides menu cards as well. Many banquet halls and restaurants do, as a matter of their fine level of service. They'll likely be printed on card stock, simply created, with the site's logo on them. (Brides who want those

Get It In Writing

IF PRINT ITEMS ARE FREE, ADD THEM TO THE CONTRACT

When you discuss these included print items with your site's planner, ask to have those details added to your contract and folder, and then e-mail the planner a confirming summary of what you discussed. That's a smart, legal way to ensure that the site knows you're on top of things and keeping your order organized. Save the legal jargon, though, and instead send a friendly message starting with: "Just recapping our chat from this morning. The place cards will be included in our plan for no extra charge, and we'll pick them up a week before the wedding. Thanks!"

fancy, hard-backed menu cards with the Swarovski crystals on their monogram pay for those and arrange for the site to display them on each table.)

Your wedding site might also hand you a stack of place-card tents for your potential use, should you not want to buy your own. They might have the site's logo and name on the inside of the tent as a promotional tool to guests, but it's likely you could live with that in exchange for the $20 or so you've saved with this freebie.

Personal Wedding Websites

There's no need to pay for the personal website where guests will access your wedding information and registries. You'll find some for-pay site hosting with lots of bells, whistles, countdowns, and videos, but you really only need a simple, basic one such as a freebie from WeddingMapper.com, a bridal website, or even some bridal registry sites. As mentioned earlier, some wedding coordinators can sweeten your deal with a free subscription to a for-pay personal site service.

Maps

Go to WeddingMapper.com to create a free account and personalize your own wedding weekend map—tagging your ceremony and reception sites and nearby coffee shops, and providing fun little FYIs like, "This is where we had our first date!" and more. Include the link to your personalized map on your wedding website, and guests can either print it out, or enter the site address on their GPS for their own free find-it.

Oh, and while you're on the WeddingMapper.com site, use the free seating chart arranging tool, as well as the other free interactive planning tools, including a budget tracker.

Speaking of seating chart planning tools and free interactive budget charts, upload the free wedding template from Microsoft OneNote to use the smart digital catchall and interactive tools that let you plan with your team, even when bridesmaids and parents live in different states.

Thank-You Notes

Sometimes thank-you notes are included in your invitations suite at no extra cost, and sometimes they're included in your photography package at no extra cost. When they're not offered as a freebie, many brides and grooms choose to hold off on ordering these until after the wedding, when they'll use some of their wedding gift money to buy elegant, beautiful thank-you notes to send to their guests.

A thank-you note always has to be in print, handwritten. This isn't a time for e-mails, e-cards, or a general thank-you shout-out on Facebook. You will find at many print companies the occasional wedding season sale that might include twenty-five free thank-you notes with your order of fifty. That's one-third for free. And many of these print sites have *other* print items they'd like you to buy for a few dollars, or will throw in for

Real Stories

STORE MEMBERSHIP PERKS
CAN EARN YOU FREEBIES

"I was so surprised by this one! I get rewards from my local office supply store when I bring in my ink cartridges to recycle. So I went to the store with $25 in free credit, and I was able to buy three packs of lovely, ecru thank-you cards and envelopes. Pays to recycle."—Evelyn, bride from Tampa

free—like a sheet of twenty-five monogrammed return address labels. That doesn't hurt.

Other Print Items

Your ceremony and reception sites likely offer additional free print items, such as driving directions, directional signs that guests follow to your ceremony spot, monogrammed or personalized cocktail napkins, and more.

Friends can also help you create your print items, with their tools and talents counting as their wedding gift to you. For instance, a friend with beautiful handwriting can write out your invitation envelopes and place cards, and a friend with a craft machine such as a Cricut Express can help make your wedding decor signs, table number cards, and other print accents.

A graphic designer friend can design your monogram as a wedding gift to you, rather than paying a pro more than $200 to design it for you. You then take that artistic JPEG and insert it on your personal wedding website, wedding programs, and other DIY print items, or submit it to your invitations designer as your official logo.

CHAPTER 8

Catering and Drinks

The food makes the wedding. It's what guests enjoy and remember most, the portion of the wedding plans that often gets the largest chunk of a wedding budget. As you've read often in this book, and will read again in the coming chapters, your site wants to impress your guests— and potentially book *their* weddings. If they *like* you, that increases your chances of a few tasty freebies even more. Catering managers just might throw in an extra cocktail party station to make your wedding even more fabulous.

You may be able to get a free course, such as a salad course, as part of the package that a caterer offers—and you may even see that the catering package includes a *free wedding cake.* More on that later.

Foods That Are Often Free

You just read that the most affordable stations for a site to throw in are hummus, pasta (one type of pasta with two types of non-meat sauces), and Asian noodles. Some other types of stations and foods that your site may be willing to give you as a freebie:

- Soup bar (vegetable soups such as potato leek are more likely than pricy lobster bisque)

- Bread bar (featuring different types of rolls and grissini)

Here's What to Say

HOW TO ASK FOR A FREE STATION

You: "Looking at the cocktail party package, would it be possible to get a hummus station added in as part of our plan?"

You've started with the polite *"Would it be possible?"* and suggested a *smart, inexpensive station.* That's key. When you ask for hummus, pasta, or an Asian noodle bar, it shows you know your catering-cost smarts, as opposed to asking for a pricier carving station, seafood, or sushi. Remember, the site has to *pay* for the food it serves at your wedding, so it can't offer freebies that will diminish its profits. An inexpensive food item is more likely to be offered.

- Risotto bar (a crowd favorite!)

- Mashed potato bar (even though it's not a new trend, guests still enjoy the creamy treat in small servings)

- Mac 'n' cheese bar (It doesn't get more crowd-pleasing than this!)

What's not likely to be offered for free? Of course, pricy meat-carving, seafood, and sushi stations, and caterers say that stations of grilled veggies and cheeses are quite expensive on the market, making it impossible to offer for free.

One *trade* you might be able to arrange is a cheese course during your meal, when you ask for guests to be served plates of thin-sliced gourmet cheese samples rather than have a big cheese cube platter at the cocktail party. Guests say that a big, cube-filled cheese platter reminds them too much of corporate parties and 1990s weddings, and they also worry about the safety of eating cheese that's been sitting out for a while. So this may be an elegant switch within your catering package.

What Else the Site Throws In for Free

Garnishing is on the house, since it's the chef's artistic presentation of dishes that really makes them wow your guests—and no reputable banquet hall, hotel, or chef is going to charge you per arugula leaf or sprig of rosemary or swirl of pomegranate sauce. Consider the garnishing to be a universal freebie from any catering site or restaurant.

Platters, pedestal plates, dozens of ceramic spoons on a platter with a bite of ceviche or mango shrimp on them, gleaming silver dishes with puff pastry appetizers on them—the artistic presentation of cocktail party fare and sit-down dinner courses is also part of the package. If a site tries to charge you for "upgraded presentation," here's what to say.

Here's What to Say

CHALLENGING A POTENTIAL CHARGE FOR GARNISHING

You: "I noticed there's a charge listed here for 'upgraded presentation.' What exactly is that?"

Chef/Manager: "It's for the extra materials and work the chef puts into garnishing, making food towers, preparing two hundred ceramic spoons with ceviche, and the last-minute fast-paced garnishing right before service."

You: "I've never heard of a site charging for that before. I've always found those things to be included in the price of the package."

And . . . stop. Just listen, because this could get good.

Chef/Manager: "I know, many of our brides and grooms are unhappy about this new policy."

Don't jump in with, "Yeah, and they tell all their friends!" You'll get the door shut on you. Give the chef time to think.

Chef/Manager: "I'll tell you what. How about I include garnishing for the foods on the stations, and have the entrée plates really garnished up nicely with sauces and leek-tied asparagus, but we'll take it easy on the hand-passed appetizers, get rid of the veggie art, and make a few other adjustments to give you *some* garnish for free?"

You: "That sounds really fair. I know your chef does a gorgeous job; that's why we chose to hire you. We're happy with this arrangement, so let's get a note in the contract so everyone remembers what we put together here."

Expert Tip: Is it nervy of you to ask for it in writing? No, it's smart. Everyone's super-busy, and you don't want to lose your free garnishing plan—even though it was a silly thing to have to negotiate for—because you didn't have the courage to write it up officially as a legal agreement.

The servers who work at the stations are a must. I spoke with celebrity wedding planner Michelle Rago, who strongly recommended getting well-trained attendants at each station who will expertly prepare and serve your foods, and keep the station looking fresh, neat, and organized with bites arranged in symmetrical lines—not picked over and smeared on the plate as guests help themselves. Don't ask for free attendants if you're presented with a charge. These pros keep the food line moving, the guests served with a smile, and the food presented beautifully and at the right temperature, with elegant, upscale, white-glove service.

And even if they are considered part of the package, provide a generous tip for them. It's just the right thing to do.

Parties That Aren't the Wedding Itself

For small gatherings such as the rehearsal dinner and the guest welcome cocktail party, the DIY trend gives everyone a financial break. While you still have to buy food to prepare—with the exception of appetizers, courses, or desserts that your co-planners will bring as their contributions to the party, free to you—there are some freebies that can add even more value to your home-cooked menu items:

- Get great recipes through top magazine websites and apps, like FoodNetwork.com, AllRecipes.com, BHG.com, and others.

- Borrow friends' and relatives' specialty cooking appliances like slow cookers, panini presses, rice makers, steamers, and grill pans. You'll now find mini pie-on-a-stick makers for creating meat- and veggie-filled hot pockets.

- Borrow friends' and relatives' chafing dishes, chip and dip sets, serving platters, bowls, and serving spoons rather than renting them.

- Take free cooking classes offered at stores like Williams-Sonoma to perfect the art of making flank steak, paninis, mini calzones, and other party fare.

- Take free classes at gourmet shops, or check YouTube and Hulu, to learn the art of garnishing food, such as making sauce swirls and onion straws.

- Find out what's free in a catering package, such as from your favorite pizza place that also caters. Some plans will provide free bread, salad, or dessert with your order, helping you afford to treat your guests to your all-time favorite menu items.

Real Stories

BRUNCHES OFFER TONS OF FREEBIES!

"We found a hotel brunch that cost $15 per person, and it had a *huge* spread of food—at least six different kinds of cold salads, shrimp cocktail, clams on the half shell, two meat carving stations, an omelet station, a full hot bar with salmon, lots of veggies, risotto, tons of breads—and at least ten different kinds of desserts. And a glass of free champagne for each guest. And free coffee. Comparing it to what it would have cost me to self-cater all of that, I figured out that everything but the shrimp cocktail and the bread was *free* . . . in theory."—Delina, bride from Nevada

A new trend in after-parties: desserts-only. If co-hosts and friends are able to bring over platters of tiramisu, cupcakes, brownies, mousses, and other desserts the night before the wedding as a potluck (which many families still embrace), your post-wedding indulgence party is all set.

The after-party menu might be leftovers brought out from the at-home rehearsal dinner you hosted the day before, or brownies, cookies, and other treats left over from the guest welcome bags. Your ultra-close friends and family will not be offended at your fridge-raid for after-party snacks and treats. Especially if what you're setting on the kitchen counter looks *gooood*.

Drinks

Top-quality drinks are not likely to be added for free to your wedding package. The site paid for those cases of wine and those top-shelf liquors, so it's unrealistic to ask for entirely free bar service. *But* your site might have a policy of including a free round of champagne for the first toast. If the site doesn't mention it, ask for it.

Here's What to Say

NEGOTIATING FOR FREE CHAMPAGNE

You: "What's your policy on the champagne toast? Is that something you include as part of the package?"

Bar Manager: "We don't normally include it, since we serve very fine champagne on our bar list. We do offer it as part of the included open bar service."

You: "Oh, then would it be possible to just have each guest given a small flute of champagne at their seats, ready for the first toast? Since they'd get it for asking at the bar anyway?"

Bar Manager: "Yes, we can arrange that."

If the site manager says, no, that champagne is an added charge, many brides and grooms just skip the pricy champagne pour and allow guests to toast them with whatever they're drinking.

As part of your open bar—never do a cash bar as a way to finagle drinks for free—choose a variety of drinks, and ask about the free ways that your bar manager plans to present them. You'll be happy to know that modern, attractive glassware is included, free to you. As is creative garnishing, like fruit spears, sugared-rims, and drop-ins like berries in those champagne flutes.

SOFT DRINKS

Most sites include soft drinks in their packages or call them free. This often includes colas, iced teas, fruit juices, club soda, and seltzers. Feel free to ask, though, for some creative serving of soft drinks—such as an Arnold Palmer, which is a mix of lemonade and iced tea. Or a seltzer-bubbled cranberry juice. Most bar managers will be happy to help you design a creative soft drinks bar list to add some pizzazz to your beverage offerings.

Here's What to Say

GETTING A SPECIFIC BAR FREEBIE

You: "My groom has mentioned a few times that he's looking forward to having a brandy with his friends at the reception, and that upgrade is over our budget. So what can we do to get that one drink option added into our existing package?"

The bar manager might suggest a swap-out such as substituting the Sambuca for the brandy to make it happen for you. If you have several specialty drink requests, your bar manager might suggest going for mid-shelf liquors while keeping the fine wine. If you don't mind the trade, this could be your groom- and crowd-pleasing freebie.

COFFEE

Most sites won't charge extra for regular coffee service, and some include cappuccino within their standard after-dinner drinks list. Want those upscale post-dinner drinks like cognac, brandy, Irish coffees, and sambuca for espresso? Just ask for an upgrade to your post-dinner drinks list.

DRINKS FOR OTHER PARTIES

When you or a friend are hosting an at-home soiree, you can grab a number of wine bottles from your own racks to serve to guests, which wine enthusiasts say is a great way to use bottles that could otherwise age and spoil. Here are some other smart freebies in the at-home drinks category:

- Ask co-planners to bring a bottle of wine or liquor as their contribution to the party.

- If you have a fully stocked bar, featuring flavored vodkas and rums, display your own supplies as your no-extra-cost bar offerings.

- Borrow a friend's margarita machine, rather than renting one.

- Borrow a large-volume coffee maker from a friend so that you're not making batches of coffee in your twelve-cup machine all night.

- Borrow pitchers from friends, rather than buying new ones or renting them, to make sangria or to serve iced tea or colas.

- Borrow ice cube containers and tongs from friends to set them on each end of your bar.

- Borrow a friend's sugar- or salt-rimmer kit to add taste and garnish to your drinks.

- Check out drink recipes for free online at FoodNetwork.com, Cocktail.com, WineSpectator.com, and other free sites. You may

Disaster!

DON'T CREATE A WINE GLASS NIGHTMARE

If you ask friends to bring over their sets of wine glasses, it can be a huge headache to figure out who owns which glasses when returning them to the rightful owners. This freebie attempt is often a big fail.

even have access to a free bar-drinks app that can provide you with spectacular drink recipes.

- Make your own ice cubes, getting creative with frozen-in mint leaves, blueberries, and other colorful add-ins. Check out free how-to videos on entertaining websites to master your ice cube art.

One freebie-hunting strategy to avoid is going without bartenders. Make room in your budget for experienced, friendly bartenders who know how to make quality drinks. If you were to ask friends to tend bar, they could easily get overwhelmed by a long line of thirsty guests, and nervous bartenders spill things. Setting out drinks for guests to help themselves could work for a small group, but if you have more than fifteen people at your party, it's a good investment to hire bartenders through your wedding coordinator, just to keep the line moving and—this is big—your liquor supply used in good measurements, not over-poured by friends, which could cause you to run out and have to go to the store for more.

CHAPTER 9

Cakes and Desserts

Is it possible to get a free wedding cake? Some reception halls and destination wedding resorts include the cake in their standard catering package, so even though it's part of the bill, you can call that a freebie!

Without a "cake and desserts included" plan, it's still possible to get *elements* of your after-dinner treats for free. Cake bakers and dessert artists want me to tell you that the creation of a cake or dessert spread costs them money—for flour, sugar, butter, berries, everything you want in a cake— and the hours of labor their workers put into your cake costs money as well, not to mention the huge costs of running that bakery with its ovens and refrigerators. They can't give you everything for free, but they're usually happy to throw in a few extras from time to time.

The Wedding Cake

Wedding cakes are so expensive because of the time and effort that go into making them. It can take a baker's team a dozen hours to make that masterpiece, with six workers spending all day handcrafting those sugar-paste daisies you want all over your cake layers. But when you ask for a simpler style of cake, perhaps an elegantly uncomplicated frosting style with just a few dozen piped pearls, your order becomes a welcome relief—and the baker just might throw in some extras.

Ask for a free flavor upgrade. Bakers have their list of regular flavors, such as vanilla, chocolate, and lemon, and then they have their list of

Real Stories

PLACE SEVERAL CAKE AND DESSERT ORDERS AT ONCE

"When a client comes in ready to order *several* cakes from us at the same time—one for the engagement party, one for the bridal shower, one for the rehearsal dinner, and one for the wedding—I'm definitely going to give them some freebies." —Angelo, baker

"upgrade" flavors available for a higher charge. If you ask for red velvet at the price of their regular flavors, you get the difference for free. The same goes for fillings. Some bakers will throw in a rum buttercream filling as a free upgrade.

Some bakers will add an extra layer to your cake for free if you order a three-layer cake. Some bakers will also offer free icing flowers if you choose not to have sugar-paste or fondant flowers or other time-consuming decorations on your cake.

Ask for extra fondant left over from your cake's layering to be cut into little shapes, like butterflies or hearts, and used as free accenting on one or several layers.

A popular freebie right now is a cake topper, and modern designs are so much cuter than those plastic brides and grooms you saw on your grandparents' cake. Some bakeries will give you a fantastic topper that's a monogram of your new last name. You can use it on this cake, or save it for another cake during your wedding weekend.

A friend may offer to make your wedding cake, but only trust this to someone who has proven experience, ideally someone who runs her own bakery or cupcakery.

THE GROOM'S CAKE

- Some bakeries will give you a free, small groom's cake if your wedding cake is elaborate.

- A friend or a relative who makes gorgeous cakes could make the groom's cake as her wedding gift to you.

- Use those craft store gift cards to get cute cake accents for your DIY groom's cake.

Additional Desserts

Here's a little secret from inside wedding world: Reception site owners want their dessert offerings to impress you and your wedding guests. So if you're only getting a wedding cake, they may be very likely to throw in an extra dessert platter, station, or even the entire big-budget dessert bar. "I want the bride and groom to love their wedding day, and be thrilled with the desserts, and there's also going to be over 150 people here for this wedding. I want them to have my dessert chefs' amazing food as well. You

Real Stories

SOME DESSERTS ARE PRICIER THAN OTHERS

"The site caterer said he'd throw in chocolate-covered strawberries with the cake, and we asked if he'd do petit fours instead. He said that petit fours take a lot of time to make, so unfortunately, no. But he was willing to do gourmet brownie squares for us."—Ellie, bride from New York City

never know. Maybe one or two of those guests will book a wedding with us," says one reception hall manager from New York City.

Some reception sites will offer free chocolate-covered strawberries if you opt to get just the cake and not the full dessert spread. Again, the site owner knows that guests want more than one dessert option, and this is an inexpensive option for them to add on when you're on a budget.

Keep in mind that seasonal desserts, such as apple tarts in the fall, are more likely to be added in for free, as these dishes are inexpensive for the site to make. And some kitchens have lots of extra fruit on hand, perhaps some mango left over from the mango and shrimp appetizer at your cocktail hour, allowing them to offer a tropical fruit salad or tropical fruit tartlets for free on your dessert bar. Sites that make their own wedding cakes often offer cake pops—which are made from leftover cake mixed with frosting, rolled into a ball, and dipped in chocolate—for free, as a smart way to use leftover cake materials they would otherwise dispose of, and they may even have a supply of chocolate truffles that they use to decorate other couples' wedding cakes, yours for the asking.

Ice cream bars may be counted as an inexpensive dessert station for the site to offer, since toppings are budget-friendly, but expect to pay more for Belgian waffles and other common dessert bar features.

If you offer to skip the been-there-done-that chocolate fountain, you could negotiate to serve all of those fruits, cookies, rum cake squares, and other "dippers" as your cut-price dessert, or trade the chocolate fountain entirely for a dessert option—such as a buffet of chocolate mousses or pastries. While this is more of an equal trade than a freebie, you could essentially get one of your or your groom's special request desserts without paying extra.

Presentation is a key factor for a great dessert spread, and a great freebie that the site will provide is a lovely display. Ask about the site's gorgeous pedestals, silver platters, cupcake stands, and other presentation stylings to make your desserts look amazing.

Real Stories

CRAFT STORE GIFT CARDS TO THE RESCUE!

"I asked for gift cards to my favorite craft store for my birthday and Christmas gifts, and I used those to get all of the cake-making supplies and cupcake decorations we'd need for free!"—Maria, bride from Minneapolis

Cakes and Desserts for Your At-Home Parties

DIY cakes and desserts are top trends for at-home parties such as your engagement party, bridal shower, rehearsal dinner, and morning-after breakfast. A talented friend or relative could make a great cake, cupcakes, cake pops, or other desserts as her shower or wedding gift to you for these events, with much less risk than for the wedding cake itself.

Additional Tips

- Use a gift card to buy premade sugar-paste flowers at the craft store, and then use those as free decorations on a plain sheet or round cake you buy or make.

- Allow close friends and family to bring their own special recipe desserts to your engagement party, bridal shower, rehearsal dinner, or morning-after breakfast as their contribution to the party. Some bridesmaids offer to make up their share of the bridal shower party costs by baking some desserts in barter.

- Take free cake-decorating classes at your local craft store, bakery, or cupcakery, where a dessert craft expert will instruct you on sugar-flower placement and other methods.

- Look to YouTube and on BHG.com for free tutorials on cake and cupcake decorating, and learn how to make and decorate your own desserts.

- Follow your favorite bakers' and cupcake designers' Facebook pages so that you can enter their contests, and you might win a cake or cupcakes for free.

- Ask to borrow friends' pedestal plates and cupcake trees for your self-hosted pre- and post-wedding parties, rather than buying or renting them.

CHAPTER 10

Florals and Decor

Since the vendor needs to buy loads of flowers and greenery, and since hours of labor are involved in creating your floral pieces, it's unlikely you'll get sizable freebie offers here. But there's always room for a few small freebies in your florals.

The smartest way to get florals and gorgeous greenery for free? Book your wedding at a site that already has them. A location that offers you the use of its gardens and grounds for an outdoor wedding, or even just for your cocktail party, is decorated by Mother Nature on her dime. You might not have to spend a cent, with all of those rose arbors and tropical plants, or daisies, tulip borders, and flowering trees in full bloom. Or, if you're having a beach wedding, the scenery and sunset alone provide the perfect decor.

One floral designer I spoke to said that when a bride books her for day-of coordination as well as her floral design, she throws in all of her team's setup for free, a value of $300. Another floral designer said that she likes to give the moms wristlets for free as part of a bridal package, when the couple is ordering more than three bouquets and more than ten centerpieces.

Free Flowers and Greenery

If a floral designer has a big order in addition to yours on your wedding weekend, you might get the benefit of her overflow. If she has a few dozen

Real Stories

PICTURE WINDOWS SET THE SCENE

"We found a place with huge, floor to ceiling picture windows overlooking the beach and the ocean. So we were still able to have an indoor wedding, with that amazing scenery. All I needed were a few little floral centerpieces for decor, so I count that as 90% free!"—Lila, bride from Tampa

extra calla lilies, she might add them to your altar decor or to your sweetheart table centerpiece. Sometimes she knows this ahead of time, and sometimes she'll just add it in last minute *because she likes you.*

Or, perhaps she'll use *your* extra flowers and greenery, left over from your bouquets and site decor, to quickly handcraft little freebie accents to your card birdcage, guest book table, the sweetheart table, and other visual points of interest. I spoke to several top-name wedding coordinators who said they like to use every single bloom, branch, and garland length to accent *something* in the wedding space, since it's the littlest details that add up to a big-budget effect. Some coordinators even bring extra glass vases with them, at no charge, to make additional floral arrangements to set around the room. These freebies add up to more than $120 worth of floral accenting, if not more.

Speaking of vases, your bridesmaids' bouquets can be set in glass vases to serve as table centerpieces or room decor, adding up to $100 in freebies, and they can also be used to decorate a mantel or the space around the wedding cake, the space behind your guest book table, and your family wedding photo display.

DIY FLORAL FREEBIES

Since DIY is all the rage, sign up for a free centerpiece-making class at your craft store or florist shop, and save on pricy labor fees by making your own simple centerpiece designs, such as all-white roses or an array of spring blooms. For further freebies, you might take some flower cuttings from your own garden (or from a relative's or friend's garden) to use in your simple decor projects. One smart freebie project is floating a self-picked flower in a water-filled glass vase you already own. This could be a table accent for your engagement party, or the flower on your remembrance table. Freshly cut flowers can also be used as lovely little accents for napkin rings or place cards, and fresh-snipped holly from your own garden can be freebie decor for your winter wedding's floral accents. (Do so carefully, though, to avoid the disaster of being all scratched up by branches on your wedding day. Also, watch out for overpruning, which could damage or kill the tree.)

If you'd rather leave your wedding day florals to the pros, but DIY your pre- and post-wedding parties, ask your floral designer if you can visit

Disaster!

THIS FLOWER FREEBIE IS NOT WORTH THE RISK!

Never cut wildflowers from the side of the road. Some are actually poisonous, and some may trigger allergies you never knew you had and could bother your guests. This is one freebie it's not worth risking, especially since some wildflowers don't smell very good when cut and placed indoors.

her design studio to pick up any leftover flowers or greenery she'd otherwise throw away. You'd be shocked at the number of perfectly pretty rose heads, leftover lacy ferns, and especially flower petals you could request for your own prewedding party use.

So many brides have told me they tried to grow their own flowers in terra-cotta pots, but it took so much time and effort, and half the flowers didn't grow very well, while some leaves got a fungus. They wound up buying florals after all of that time and effort, not to mention lots of wasted money.

What *does* work? Showing off your own potted orchids and green plants at your at-home party. If there's a pretty green ivy plant in the bedroom, bring it down as a decor piece for the engagement party.

Decor Items

Your floral designer probably has a storeroom filled with leftover decor items that she hasn't gotten around to using and can't return to her supplier. She may, if you ask, allow you to use them in your decor plans. These items include: crystals, mini glass vases, pedestal platters, branches, LED light cubes to place in your centerpieces, and lengths of lace and ribbon.

SEASONAL DECOR ITEMS

What's the season of your wedding? And what can you find out there in nature that's free for the taking? Don't forget that friends and family may have seasonal decor items to lend you, as well:

- Spring and Summer: Hand-collected stones from a riverbed, lake, or ocean; hand-collected sea glass if you get that on your shores and collect over time; daisy-print ribbon; bright-hued ribbon; an extra bolt of brightly hued fabric.

- Fall: Hand-collected pinecones are the big one. Ask friends and bridal party members to pick up pinecones for you on their properties or during their travels. Currently popular are little glass centerpieces filled with free acorns, gathered by friends before the wedding.

- Winter: Ask if anyone can lend you their decor strings of faux cran-berries, or Christmas decor plastic icicles, strings of white or col-ored lights, or collections of solid-colored ornaments that can be displayed on also-borrowed platters as entirely free centerpieces. Use the ice theme of winter by making your own ice rings and ice plat-ters in your freezer and then using them in punch bowls and as serv-ing platters, covered by lettuces or fresh spinach for a pretty look.

This tip was just featured on the HGTV *Home by Novogratz* show: "Fabric stores always have extra fabric they'd like to get rid of." You don't have to be a famous interior designer to score craft-worthy bolts of fabric or short lengths of lace, shimmer ribbon, or other accent items. You might be able to get some freebies thrown in with your runner fabric order.

Real Stories

HIT THE RIBBON FREEBIE JACKPOT

"We scored tons of great ribbon from some of our relatives. Everyone has tons of leftover ribbon from their holiday gift-wrapping, and I knew my mom had some gorgeous silver ribbon on spools. So we asked if we could help clean out their leftovers, and they let us! We made our pew ribbons and centerpiece ribbon accents for free. And while we were scavenging for ribbon, we also found packets of wine-colored beads that we used as accents on our menu cards and place cards."—Elizabeth, bride from Chicago

On the House

Use what the site has on hand for free. Most sites will allow you to pick out tablecloth colors from their "included" palette, but they'll charge extra if you want tablecloths in designer colors or shimmery fabrics. Add some shimmer on your own by asking if you can bring in your own table runners that an aunt, grandmother, sister, or friend easily makes for you, and lay those across the ivory-colored tablecloths for a pop of shimmer and shading.

Many top-name wedding coordinators responded to my request for freebie tabletop design ideas with the advice to choose a darker-colored linen, such as deep cranberry, hunter green, sapphire, deep purple, chocolate, even black, from the site's free offerings, since light-colored plates and flowers really pop in contrast to them. And it doesn't cost a penny.

Ask the site what its already-taken-care-of decor items are. Many brides find out that the site provides low-set centerpieces on the cocktail party tables, so they don't have to order them, or lighting effects, like a pin light on the cake table.

Get It In Writing

ALWAYS GET YOUR COLOR CHOICE IN WRITING

When you decide on your linen colors, have it noted in your contract that you've selected color number *X* for your *free* tablecloth, napkins, cake table, guest book table, and all other specific tables where those linens will go. You have to be super-specific in your legal contract to ensure you get the freebies you arranged. And when you call to confirm a few days before the wedding, clarify that you're getting the sapphire linens, not the ivory ones.

Most sites have couches, ottomans, and high-low tables and chairs that you can ask to use to turn your rehearsal dinner or cocktail party into a clubby atmosphere without having to rent those furniture pieces. Some sites will even wheel a grand piano into the room just for effect.

Learn How To for Free

Craft stores always have a long list of how-to DIY classes, teaching everything from making ribbon bows at Christmastime (take the class now, and use the lessons for your summer wedding) to decorating greeting cards (take that class, and use the lesson on your place cards). These free classes provide you with skills you'll use for all of your wedding parties, and also for parties in the future.

Another great source for how-to crafts is a video site like YouTube or Hulu. The free video sites are a mecca for DIY lessons.

Floral designers also give classes at their shops, but those aren't usually free. They might be a great thing to ask for as a gift, though, especially if the class fee includes a discount or freebie for your wedding floral designs.

Real Stories

BECOME YOUR OWN WORD ARTIST

"I went online to find calligraphy font styles and used a regular pen to practice making those swirly writing designs. I used a gift card to the office supply store to get a calligraphy pen and some card stock, and made my own guest welcome basket cards, place cards, and thank-you notes."—Nina, bride from Boston

And Then There's the Borrow

Your friends and family will likely be happy to lend you their glass vases, pedestal platters, photo frames for the family photo table, even digital photo frames to play a slide show of images, with their contributions counting as their wedding gifts to you. They'll love helping you achieve your wedding dream, and they'll also love getting a big financial break on your gift.

Other items that brides say they've borrowed include: the gift envelope birdcage or box, the fancy pen for the guest book, holiday wreaths, easels and stands for portraits and signs, platters for displaying wedding favors, specialty table linens like a pearl-studded round for the cake table, strings of holiday lights, holiday ornaments, kids' sand buckets and shovels for beach party decor, floral wreaths, and more.

CHAPTER 11

Photography and Videography

I f there's any place you'd *want* a freebie, it's the ultra-expensive photography and videography category. Both, after all, can cost more than $2,000 per package—perhaps triple that in some regions of the country— and a single parents' album can cost more than $300. But if there's any place you *shouldn't* go too far for a freebie, it's right here.

Your wedding photos and video are *extremely* important. They're the only parts of your wedding day that stay with you, capturing all the magic of your Big Day—including moments you didn't even see, like your grandparents doing the cha-cha while you were mingling with friends—and they grow priceless over time. Entrusting your wedding photos and video to a friend for free, to save money, is probably the worst decision you can make. Let that friend shoot photos at your engagement party or rehearsal dinner, but make sure pros handle your wedding day images and video.

There *are* some freebies to be had here, and I've got the inside scoop from the top wedding photographers and videographers in the country:

Photography

When you're paying for a professional photography package, what you're getting for free, essentially, is the photographer's years of experience, trained eye, ability to be everywhere at once, top-notch shooting and editing equipment, and the ability to round up your distracted bridal party

That's Going to Cost You

DON'T BOOK A PRETENDER

Booking the cheapest photographer out there is going to cost you in the long run. These days it seems as if any person with a camera can call himself a photographer, but wedding photography is an art. A true, accredited pro who belongs to elite associations and charges more because his work is *worth* it is your smarter budget strategy. Talk to your recently married friends, wedding coordinator, floral designers, and other pros to find out who's good out there. They know the difference between the pros and the pretenders.

and child attendants to get those group portraits done after the ceremony in record time. It's the intrinsic gifts of the photographer that you can count as the top freebie here.

A pro, for instance, will give you a free consultation. You meet with him or her, look through sample albums and slide shows, discuss the details of your wedding plans, share your wedding style, and tell him or her *you're on a budget.* This free meeting sets the foundation for a great working relationship. And great rapport often leads to better results, and perhaps some nice freebies.

Within the photography package, and with your prints and albums, there are a number of great freebies popping up in the industry, some that can save you hundreds of dollars. And don't forget that photographers often offer those gift cards, which can be a terrific wedding present from parents, grandparents, and other special loved ones.

PACKAGE DEALS

When you look at the photographer's budget, silver, gold, and platinum packages, each with a certain numbers of proofs and albums, you may see a larger number of free items listed within the pricier packages. That's just good business on his part, making that $3,000 or higher package more attractive to you. And indeed it may be, when you do the math and see that free albums add up to more than $600 in savings. So don't look past the pricier packages. There may be a free photo booth in them for you.

Looking at the budget package can be your strategy, and *asking* for some freebies is still within your reach. As mentioned earlier, when a photographer likes you, he or she may be happy to throw in some add-ons.

Some things can nudge a photographer into offering you freebies, such as their wanting to shoot at the great venue you booked. Photographers know that lots of brides out there would rather book an expert who has experience at the reception hall where their wedding will take place. If your wedding gives them the chance to say, "I shot at the Terrace Gardens," they get an important credit that can lead to more business down the road.

What to Expect

THE ART OF THE DEAL

If a photographer says that your wedding could be shown in a bridal magazine, don't take that as license to say, "Oh, so you'll get thousands of dollars worth of exposure through us, so let's eliminate your charge!" That's going too far. Just be flattered and know that you're on the right track to establish a positive, respectful relationship with your photo pro. That's your goal right now and could lead to additional freebies later.

They also want to shoot cultural weddings, perhaps featuring some of your wedding on their site or blog to "sell" themselves to a wide wedding audience. That could be worth thousands to them down the road, so they don't mind giving you an extra free hour on your package or a free proof book worth $150.

Photographers know what the local bridal magazine editors are looking for in editorial spreads and for cover shots, so if they see potential in your outdoor or rooftop wedding, they may reward you for being their saving grace with some free prints or enlargements or a signature frame worth $150.

The next big topic is the number of hours in the package. Most photographers agree that for them to capture all of the most important elements of your day, including the hours before the ceremony, the ceremony itself, and the special moments of the reception, they need enough hours. They may say that five hours is the absolute minimum that would work for your plans, and they're more comfortable with seven. "I don't want the bride rushed around to get group photos, and have to push up her cake cutting because I have to leave," says one photographer from Washington, D.C. So be sure that the package you choose includes enough time, so that you're not losing your pro or paying overtime. A pro *may* throw in an extra hour on your package if you ask nicely, or he may agree to stay an hour later without charging you overtime. "These are things I do for wedding couples I *like*," says our D.C. photo pro.

Within the package, you'll likely see that the photographer includes the services of his assistants. This is *not* an element to try to negotiate out as a way to save—even if it's the $30 meal for that assistant at the reception. On-scene assistants are priceless; they allow the photographer to focus on shooting *you* before the wedding while *they* take care of setting up the lighting equipment, camera tripods, and more at the ceremony. They're also well-trained "shooters" who can get the guys' portraits while

That's Going to Cost You

WINNING YOUR PHOTOGRAPHER COULD BE A LOSING PROSPECT

While many top-level pros offer prizes of free photography at bridal shows, some novices and shady pros attend them, too. So if you win free photography at an expo, always research the experts carefully, see which professional associations they belong to, and check out their samples. If they don't check out, don't accept the deal.

the main photographer shoots you and your girls getting ready. So if assistants are in the package, consider their support work to be worth every penny if there's an extra charge or a priceless freebie if they're included.

Ask plenty of questions about the type of photography offered. "If a photographer attempts to charge you for HD photography, find another photographer," says one expert from New Jersey, who says the same goes for videography. "It's the professional's job to upgrade his equipment and offer you the best quality possible."

Ask to negotiate out any elements of the package that you don't want. For instance, if you don't plan to order $300 parents' albums, but that's in the package, ask to have that element removed and either discounted from your bill (to give you money to use on something else, which would make that something else free) or replaced by a different item, such as a $150 proof album.

ENGAGEMENT PORTRAITS

Many professional photographers now offer engagement sessions for free, which they say allows them to get to learn more about you, your

That's Going to Cost You

DON'T BE IN A RUSH

Be patient when it comes to getting your edited photos and video. Same-day or rush editing costs an extra $300 on average, according to TheWeddingReport.com. If you're willing to wait a few weeks, you free up that $300 for other purchases.

photography style, your best angles, and your wedding. Pros say they don't want the first time they work with you to be on your wedding day. This service used to cost more than $200 in some areas, so consider this a delightful freebie, and photos from your engagement session could wind up on your invitations and programs as free design elements.

EDITING

Digital effects such as black-and-white, sepia, or black-and-white with a single color pop are usually free, since it doesn't take a photo editor long to produce these effects. Ask if effects are free before you request them, and ask to have them for free if the package doesn't specify.

PRINTS

Some photographers include a small number of free prints in their packages. For instance, you might get a free bride and groom 11 x 14 inch portrait included in the price of your package or six free 5 x 7's in your order from the photographer's online gallery.

You might also find, or negotiate, a free flip book of 3 x 5 inch photos, and—my favorite—free print proofs of your wedding photos. These are actual printed pictures that you've selected from the photographer's online gallery, which the photographer will have developed and printed *without editing*, so you can look through them to pick your finals for your albums. Yes, many pros show wedding proofs online in password-protected galleries

Here's What to Say

HOW TO ASK FOR FREE PRINT PROOFS

If your photographer's package doesn't include the option of free print proofs, this script may be able to help you get a big, valuable freebie just for the asking.

You: "Do you offer print proofs as part of this package?"

Photographer: "We *can* do print proofs, but most of our brides prefer to see their proofs in a proof book."

You: "We'd really like to have individual print proofs, so can we get a collection of those as part of our package?"

Photographer: "I can give you print proofs rather than the proof book, if you'd like. But most of our couples like having the book to have all of their proofs right there."

You: "We're fine with skipping the book and just looking online, then getting the print proofs if we can work that out."

Photographer: "We can work that out."

Keep in mind that a proof book costs an average of $168, so the print proofs are an even trade, but *then* become freebies for you as more than $1,000 worth of free framed photos and albums.

to cut down on their developing costs or having a proof book created, but you'll still find great pros who give these freebie prints. If so, you have one hundred or so freebies that you can frame for yourself, for your parents, grandparents, and bridal party members, or use to create albums for your closest friends and family. It's a savings of thousands of dollars in free prints and album material.

Also in the photographer's print package may be free wallet-size photos for your thank-you notes, which is a savings of more than $40 in many cases. If you don't see them as a free offer, ask for them to be free, especially if you'll order additional prints or framed portraits.

Speaking of framed portraits, a wonderful gift given to the bride and groom by parents, grandparents, godparents, and bridal parties is an 11 x 14 inch framed wedding portrait. It's a forever-keepsake, often a few hundred dollars, and a fabulous gift from loved ones. All you have to do is tell your family and friends that you would love *that* as a gift. And of course, parents love getting a fabulous 8 x 10 inch or 11 x 14 inch framed portrait as their thank-you gift as well. If you're placing a good-size order with your

That's Going to Cost You

PRINTING OUT YOUR OWN PHOTOS ISN'T A FREEBIE "WIN"

It might seem like a great freebie to just print out friends' photos on your home computer and printer, using glossy photo printing cards from the office supply store, but that process uses a *lot* of ink. An ink cartridge can cost more than $40, and you could burn out several color ink cartridges if you print out many photos. Add in the cost of photo card stock, and this becomes *far* from a freebie.

photographer, you may be able to negotiate free framing—or use that craft store gift card to buy a beautiful frame for free, just for this gift.

ALBUMS

Some packages include free albums for the parents, which amounts to a $600 freebie, and you can also give your parents the free flip book if you're giving them a framed portrait as well. No matter who's getting your free album, keep in mind that the greatest expense goes to editing and layout. Here's a smart freebie secret from a photography pro in New York City: If you tell your photo editor that you'd like a duplicate of your album design for your parents, that can make editing *free* for theirs, and you just pay a smaller amount for the album itself.

When ordering your album, ask which elements are free, such as squared album pages, and which cost extra, such as rounded album page

Real Stories

IT MAY BE SMART TO SKIP THE ALBUMS FOR RIGHT NOW

Since albums are so pricy, and since freebies may be hard to come by in this category, some couples skip them for right now, opting to just get their images on disk and planning to order albums for themselves and their parents months down the road. "I have it in my contract that wedding couples can take two years to order their albums," says one photographer from New York City. "It's my 'concession to the recession,' and I find that I get more album orders in the long run when couples know they don't have to order them *now*."

corners. Ask for free monogramming, which is often thrown in, and ask about the different materials in which albums come. Leather albums are among the priciest, so don't expect that as your freebie; but you might be able to negotiate an album upgrade from basic vinyl to a pretty canvas design.

PHOTOS FROM FRIENDS

Friends who attend the wedding will send you plenty of photos that you can edit on your own using Photoshop to remove red-eye or crop, or even use the slimming feature. If you have a friend with photo-editing experience, perhaps he or she can edit some images for you, again as a wedding gift. These images, from your wedding day as well as from other wedding parties and events, might become your freebie favorites, as well as frame-able gifts for parents and bridal party members.

If you'd like to print any of these from the photo-share site your friend uses, like Shutterfly or Snapfish, keep an eye out for these sites' three-cent print sales, which would add up to several dozen free prints compared to regular print fees. With a RetailMeNot.com coupon code, you could get even more for free, plus free shipping.

ADDITIONAL FREEBIE-HUNTING STRATEGIES

- Befriend your photographer on Facebook and Twitter to catch any announcements of his special sales on prints, or a free brag book, or even a contest for all free albums.

- Ask if your photographer will give you a Mess the Dress session for free if you keep it local. A Mess the Dress, or Trash the Dress, session takes place after the wedding, and you either wear your own wedding dress or a second bridal dress to be captured splashing in the ocean surf, jumping into a pool, laying down with your groom in autumn leaves, or dancing in the rain—anything artistic in which your dress gets messy, to pretty effect.

- If you do rent a photo booth, ask if the company provides free, fun props for guests to use, or ask friends to bring some of their Halloween costume accessories like feather boas, pirate hats and eye patches, baseball hats, and more for free props.

- Ask if you can arrange free delivery and pickup of the photo booth. Many photographers will allow for this $75 charge to be wiped from a contract.

- Arrange your own *free* photo booth by setting up a little corner with a colored background, props you've collected yourself, and either one-time-use cameras set by the area or a friend with a camera taking photos during the dessert hour only.

- Check out your smartphone's apps. Yours may have the ability to take photos and print them out in photo booth-strip format. Yours doesn't? Ask if a friend has that app installed.

- Set up a digital photo frame you already own on the family photos table, and display a slide show of your relatives' weddings, or make it an "all about us" slide show featuring images of the two of you.

Real Stories

PHOTO SLIDE SHOWS ARE NOT JUST FOR THE RECEPTION

"We displayed a digital photo frame with pictures of us at the rehearsal dinner. Best of all? The digital photo frame was a gift from our bridal shower, so the whole thing was totally free."—Amie, bride from New Jersey

Videography

The video is priceless. It shows the beauty and action of your day, and in the future, that footage of your grandparents, parents, and other loved ones will be incredibly valuable. Don't ask Uncle Charlie to take the video. Go with a steady-handed, eagle-eyed expert who may be willing to throw in some free elements.

A true, accredited, experienced videographer is crucial for the quality of your video footage and editing, and successful video pros are able to grant some freebies since their businesses are doing so well. Still, this is an art, requiring expensive equipment and lots of editing time, so don't expect thousands of dollars in free videography services and products. If you get some pieces of this category for free, that's a valuable "win" in your freebie hunt.

PACKAGE DEALS

Assess the different packages to see which one gives you what you want. Again, a higher-level plan with a pricier fee may offer more in the way of freebies, but you might not want an hour-long edited video. For many couples, a twenty-minute finished product is just fine.

If you see the option of one-, two-, or three-camera shooting, which gives you different angles in your finished video and captures more details on the big day, be aware that you usually won't get the extra "shooter" (second video pro) for free, since that shooter has to be paid. You might find out, when you ask, that your videographer has an intern who can shoot with him at no extra charge. That might even be part of a special budget package.

One freebie you may have great luck in arranging is a video montage presentation at the start of the reception. If you don't see it, and can't negotiate it, have a friend edit your childhood and courtship photos to music and just hand it to your entertainers to play for free.

Real Stories

You Could Get a Free Second Shooter

"I make money teaching videography to novices who are on the way up, so I may bring in one of my star students to get real-wedding experience, and not charge the bride and groom."—Barry, videographer

EDITING

Editing is where the videographer spends most of his time, so he's *not* going to give you a full edit for free. Instead, ask for the raw video coverage, which is the unedited footage he shoots on the wedding day. He shoots, and you score a full-length master video on DVD *that you can have edited later.*

Another option, free for you and a big budget break for them when you make it your wedding gift, is to ask a friend who's very experienced

Get It In Writing

Ask for a Short Starter Video

You might get your videographer to edit a short video set to one song that you can show your friends and family right now, with a clause in your contract that you have a year to get your video edited professionally. Be sure that your contract specifies the exact date ranges, usually from the date of your wedding, and the length of the video he or she will create.

Disaster!

DON'T LOSE YOUR WEDDING FOOTAGE

Always copy your raw or master DVD first, and then give the copy to anyone who will be editing your video for you. You don't want your master footage to get destroyed from a computer malfunction, a spilled beverage, or other danger. And when you get your edited DVD, copy it for viewing and store the master in a fireproof safe.

in video editing—maybe he works in the business—to edit your master wedding DVD.

SPECIAL EFFECTS

Stick with effects that are free, such as black-and-white, silk or soft focus, or slow-motion. These don't take your expert long to incorporate into the edit and should be free of charge. Skip the trendy special effects such as neon flashing lights and other "look what my computer can do" effects. Your video stays elegant and lovely without them. Some videographers may offer you one or two special effects, such as fade-ins and fade-outs that his apprentice will create as practice, giving you a slightly edited video for no extra charge. Ask if your videographer would consider that, and you might just plant a great idea.

COPIES

Most videographers will include two to five free copies of the wedding video in their standard packages, and videographers say they'll offer a few additional copies to couples who have been great to work with.

Another freebie to request is a podcast version of your wedding video, for posting on Facebook, YouTube, or your personal wedding website. Most experts will be happy to re-encode a brief section of your video and let you have it for free. Video experts say that this is an easy and non-time-consuming task they're most likely to offer as a freebie when asked.

As for designer jewel cases in which to keep your wedding DVD, this too is something that many professional videographers will throw in for free, sometimes as a surprise when they send your completed video. If you find that this is a pricy, for-pay offering, it's quite easy to make your own. Friends may even have extra jewel cases and DVD labels they would be willing to give you, or they may even design the label for you. Recently married friends often have supplies for this left over from when they made their own video labels, so start your search there.

CHAPTER 12

Transportation

Brides and grooms who choose one location for their weddings, conducting both the ceremony and reception in one spot, often skip transportation altogether. They eliminate the pricy cost of limousines and just have a friend drive them in a decorated convertible or in their own cleaned-and-waxed car.

If you plan to skip the vehicle rental in favor of being driven in a friend's car, you also eliminate the expensive extras of overtime fees—it can be easy to stay longer than expected at your reception, miss the 11 p.m. departure time, and rack up hundreds of dollars in overtime fees, as well as a generous tip for the driver. The friend who drives you does so as his wedding gift to you, which makes everyone a freebie winner.

If you do decide to rent a limousine or classic car, you can arrange some freebies by asking for them, even if you don't see them on the limousine company's official wedding package lists. For instance, you could negotiate an extra hour in trade for getting a smaller, non-stretch limousine or one without the mood lighting and satellite TV inside, or you could get free snacks and water inside the limo, which is just asking for a $20 or so charge to be wiped off your bill. Most companies are happy to do so. And it's great to have that ice cold water waiting for you when you get in your limo for the ride to the reception.

Another common freebie with limousine companies is a red carpet rolled out in front of the car door for your approach as husband and wife.

Get It In Writing

ADD THOSE LIMO FREEBIES TO YOUR CONTRACT

Any freebie that you request, and that the limo rental agent agrees to, needs to be written into your contract at the time of agreement. Do this in person, asking the agent to write the note specifically in his handwriting and initial it. Be specific about wording, too: "Extra hour in place of eliminated champagne, return time now midnight," for example. Smile, shake hands, and the deal is done.

Some companies charge $40 for this, but you can often arrange to add this for free, especially if you wave off their bridal package offer of a bottle of champagne and a champagne stand by the car door.

Watch out for this shady charge, and ask for it to be excised from your contract: There should be no charge for pre-wedding car cleaning and waxing. Believe it or not, some companies will slap you with a $100 service charge for making their car shiny and pretty, so read that contract well, ask what the service charge is, and negotiate it out, reasoning that it's a reflection on the company to have a sleek and shiny car in front of all your guests.

The hotel where your wedding reception is taking place might have its own limousines, for use by VIP guests. Ask if you might be able to score a free ride from the ceremony back to the hotel. This freebie is most often given when you've booked a sizable wedding or blocked a lot of rooms for guests, but it can't hurt to ask even if you haven't qualified as a platinum wedding.

And ask your wedding coordinator if he or she has any partnerships with limousine or classic car companies. Very often, wedding pros run in packs of loyal friends, and your coordinator could make one call to her buddy with the Bentley to snag you a free hour, half the overtime fee if needed, and that red carpet.

Other Types of Car Rentals

If you plan to rent a convertible or classic car, look to the special member-ships you may have through work or your professional associations that can—by virtue of a partnership with your company or group—offer you a free upgrade of car style, or even an extra day of use at no charge. There are perks to membership, and many people don't even realize that they *have* these benefits available to them. Also, many car rental companies are try-ing to stay afloat in this economy by offering an extra day, or extra hours, in their rental plan. If you don't see such an offer on their site, call them and ask if you can have it. They may prefer to get your business than have you go elsewhere.

A great resource for car rental deals is your region's tourism office (find yours at TOWD.com.) In an effort to boost large-group tourism, these offices are often granted special coupons for vehicle rentals, includ-ing a free extra day or a car upgrade to a snazzier model. Within the travel industry, special attention is given to making guests' lives easier, so you might find that a hotel offers not just discounted room blocks but freebies in car rentals for guests, and you can snag one of those deals for your own classic car rental, if you ask. The concierge might have general car rental freebies and perks, if you check at that counter as well, identifying your-self as a wedding couple with a room block. Concierges have limousine company connections that could easily get you an entirely free limo rental.

If you're planning a destination wedding that would require your guests to rent a car for travel around an island or locale, check the airline's special wedding packages for group discount fares that may also include a free car rental.

Hotel membership cards are great resources for extra freebies in many categories, and they too might offer you discounts and freebies on car rentals, as do credit card reward cards.Check the professional associations you belong to, to see if your card-carrying status can get you a free weekend, day, or upgrade. Even some corporations have employee perk offers, including transportation breaks and deals. Visit your HR office to see what you might be eligible for.

Additional Transportation Freebies

Your hotel is one of the best sources for free transportation, for your guests as well as for you. Most hotels and resorts offer free use of their shuttle buses—not just to and from the airport, but also for your group's use in getting to the ceremony, then to the reception, and back to the hotel (if the reception isn't *at* the hotel). Some establishments reserve their shuttle fleet for their brides and grooms with receptions taking place in their own ballrooms, so be aware of that condition if you're *not* having your reception on the hotel's property.

If you don't see "free use of our shuttle services" in your wedding package, ask for it. Most hotels will be happy to oblige. And with their services, you won't need to rent limousines for your family members to get to the ceremony and reception, either. Some brides and grooms choose to forgo the private ride from the reception to the hotel, via pricy limousine, and hop on board the hotel shuttle with their guests and bridal party members. It may be your free ride to the after-party in the hotel lounge, and it's certainly a fun way to travel with your festive friends and family.

If you're planning a destination wedding, check your package carefully for the term "transfer charge," which means the resort charges a fee for your guests, and you, to take its ferry or shuttle to the resort. If yours is a destination wedding of more than thirty people, you have better leverage in requesting that the transfer fee be waived. But even if you're just ten people, it's still worth it to ask. Resort managers tell me that they wish they could waive wedding groups' transfer fees, but it costs so much to fuel and maintain their gleaming ferries, and to pay for their staff as well as the free rum drinks they make you on your journey, that they depend on those $50 fares to pay the charges. So if you're met with a no, that's likely why.

However, I spoke with several bed-and-breakfast owners who reward their wedding couples for booking their establishments with a free limousine ride. B&B owners have their own lists of partner companies, and this is one of many perks they may be able to arrange.

Some resorts will arrange a free ride on their seasonal transportation, such as a horse-drawn sleigh taking you one hundred yards across a snowy field to your reception, as a part of their wedding package. They know this ride provides excellent photos, and brides and grooms fall so in love with the resort that they come back year after year. All from the romance of that sleigh ride. And if you prefer a snowmobile ride? That can be arranged.

Finally, there's the walking procession. If your ceremony and reception are near to each other, you might choose to borrow an old European custom of the bride and groom leading a colorful, streamer-waving procession of wedding guests through the streets to the celebration. You'll get lots of attention and admiration from well-wishers, and your entire group gets to your destination for free.

Check out chapter 19 (page 171) for information on how to arrange to borrow a limousine or classic car ride. You may be able to trade your website design expertise or writing skills, or another valuable service, with the limo company to get a free limo for the day.

CHAPTER 13

Entertainment

The entertainment at your reception is a very important element of your wedding's success. You may have seen well-meaning budget brides online suggesting that you plug in your iPod and get your wedding entertainment for free, but that is *not* the best strategy for saving on your wedding. You would lose so much not just in sound quality (compared to what a DJ or a band provides), but also in having a live entertainment leader sensing the vibe of your partygoers, adjusting the playlist when he sees that your crowd is packing the dance floor for slower songs, or revving up the party's energy with interaction.

Great entertainment makes your reception a smash success, so don't risk the disaster of an empty dance floor, bored guests who leave early, and no great dancing photos and video when your music is obviously a cheap-out.

Yes, having a band or a DJ is pricy, and you do need to feed them at the reception—there's no cutting that out, either. But it's worth it, and most freebie-hunting brides and grooms say they're happy to "go free" with other elements of their wedding plans so that they can spend more on the entertainment, as well as other top-priority categories. It may be your goal to spend lavishly on this crucial part of your day, which would be smart.

We're not aiming for free entertainment here at your reception. The iPod plan could be ideal for your engagement party, your rehearsal dinner, even your bridal shower and morning-after breakfast. Those are where the iPod freebies work wonderfully. Here, we're looking at a few extra effects, and performances, that you may be able to get for free.

Setting the Scene

Entertainers often include within their packages the option of special lighting effects, such as "gobo lights" (die-cut forms slipped over a light to project your names, monogram, stars, or other shapes) or "light washes" (a special effect that blankets the entire room or dance floor in a particular

Here's What to Say

HOW TO ASK FOR FREE LIGHTING EFFECTS

You: "So we're all set with your five-hour package for our reception. I'm seeing a lot of entertainment companies offering light washes right now. Is that something you'd consider as an add-on to our package?"

You haven't said "freebie," and you're *asking*. You haven't said that other companies are offering it for free. You're opening a dialogue in which the vendor will ask what you have in mind. If you just want the one light wash, he may throw it in. If you want a pricy custom gobo with your monogram, you'll likely have to pay for that. Gobo lights in swirls and snowflake effects that they have on-hand? You could very well get those, if you say, "Do you have any gobos in decorative shapes that you'd be willing to project for us?" Entertainment companies may decide that the better light show they put on, the more your guests will be impressed—and maybe some guests in your crowd are looking for an entertainment group for *their* wedding.

color). An example of a great "light wash" is a golden-toned lighting effect filling the room at sunset, creating a beautiful glow. In the nighttime hours, the "light wash" can be switched to a bright orange for a clubby, exciting, electric feel.

Why am I mentioning an expensive lighting package in a book about freebies? Because this is what more entertainment companies are starting to throw in as their freebies when you book them. They already have the lighting equipment and star- or snowflake-shaped gobo circles, the color wash films, and other supplies—it doesn't cost them anything to use these at your wedding. So it's an attractive, free perk to booking them.

If they haven't made such effects part of their incentive plan, ask if you can have them.

A fun fact: Many florists will set up their own lighting effects, including light washes and pin lights set on the centerpiece florals, or they'll talk to the site manager about having the site arrange pin lighting on the guest tables, or just on the sweetheart table, and especially on the cake. Talk to your floral designer first about possible freebie lighting effects arranged by her, and ask your wedding coordinator if he or she has an industry partnership that could net you some freebies if a call can be made.

VIDEO PRESENTATIONS

If you open your reception with a video montage, your entertainment company may be your go-to source for the screens and equipment to show it. You considered this back in the Videography section, and it may be your videographer who produces your film. But it could be your entertainers who show it on their state-of-the-art equipment as part of their package. And again, they may offer this as an incentive to book them.

THE STAGE

Before you sign on for the entertainers' elevated stage, or rent one, check your site to see if it has an elevated stage or its own stage equipment. The

What to Expect

ASKING FOR A FREE VIDEO SHOWING

If you ask for a video montage-showing freebie and hear a no, it may be because a large collection of equipment and flat-screen TVs is needed to show your video; additionally, other wedding couples may have already booked their video presentation equipment for that day. This is a larger value offering and may be more likely to be thrown in as a freebie only if you have a big-ticket wedding or are a reality show star.

site might also have big, long tables that the DJ will need to set up his hefty equipment and supplies, eliminating any rental charges from your tally.

PERFORMANCES

Entertainment companies keep a long list of talented singers, musicians, trios, even acrobats and jugglers on their rosters, and big-budget weddings often include various acts and performances to make their celebrations a real show. For your wedding, you might love the idea of having a DJ but also have a live performer take the stage to do a few numbers. You could book one of the entertainment company's stellar singers, or you could give this spotlight moment to a talented friend or relative who will perform a song as a wedding gift to you.

Again, it has to be a talented artist within your circle, not something out of a high school talent show. Your stepbrother's garage band is likely not the best act for your reception. We're talking command performance-worthy acts, not a momentum-stopping, what-were-they-thinking karaoke moment that spoils this important event.

Real Stories

GIVING A LOVED ONE THE MICROPHONE

"My dad sang at my sister's wedding, and he brought down the house with his rendition of 'Fly Me to the Moon.' I'm going to have him sing the same song at my wedding, and he'll do so again when my little sister gets married. It's a new family tradition, and he couldn't be happier about how much we all love to hear him sing!"—Brianna, bride from San Diego

And as for your karaoke machine? Well, save that for pre- and post-wedding parties. Some people get too wound up, and too drunk, to perform anything well via karaoke.

STUDENT MUSICIANS

Several budget wedding guides, including my own, suggest tapping into the vast wealth of talent at a performing arts school or college to find a wonderful singer, guitarist, trio, or other act to make your wedding special. It's valuable experience for them and something they can add to their portfolios, but don't expect it to be free. Offering them the chance to perform for "exposure" is, just like with vendors, insulting, and devalues their time.

If you have leftover funds after all of your other freebie finds, it might be well worth the budget save to offer your student musician a small monetary amount, somewhere in the neighborhood of $100. But if you're looking for *free* entertainment, leave those kids alone.

The same goes for high school jazz bands, marching bands, choir groups, and other performers. You can't expect free labor from kids. Also note that the school system has to be contacted if you wish to arrange for the marching band to accompany you on your walking procession or for the school's Juilliard-bound soloist to sing at the wedding. School boards have strict rules and legalities about arranging for their students to perform anywhere. You may have a lot of hoops to jump through. And remember, it's still not free—a donation to the marching band or choir is most often a must.

Props and Extras

Entertainers often help spice up a party by handing out props that they've brought along for free. The days of the inflatable guitar are over for most entertainment companies, but your entertainers might hand out glow sticks and necklaces or other trinkets that dancing partiers can wear. Be sure to check what kinds of props your entertainers use—you may not want to include some freebies, like plastic leis, because you may not want them in all of your reception dancing photos.

Entertainment at Other Events

Besides the presence of iPods at your engagement party and rehearsal dinner, and your niece charming everyone at your shower with her flute performance, there is another category of free entertainment that you might be able to feature at your pre- and post-wedding events: musicians who perform where your party takes place.

Take the hotel's brunch, for example. The hotel might be the site of your bridal shower, or your morning-after brunch for out-of-town-guests. Very often, hotels arrange for a pianist to play a grand piano right outside the brunch area to fill the space with elegant music. Music that's free to you. It creates a lovely ambiance for your event, and you didn't have to spend an extra dime.

At the rehearsal dinner, the restaurant might have a guitarist or a band performing in the main dining room. Your group might be right there

Real Stories

EVEN PRIVATE PARTY ROOMS
PROVIDE ACCESS TO LIVE PERFORMANCES

"We chose a fabulous jazz club for our rehearsal dinner because they have a private party room downstairs, and they pipe in the music from the live performances upstairs in the main dining room. On the night of our rehearsal dinner, they had Nat King Cole's brother performing! It was amazing!"—Jenna, bride, speaking of Shanghai Jazz in New Jersey, one of the top jazz clubs in the country.

with them or able to hear them in the side party room where your group is enjoying its meal.

And finally, if your party is at home, you might simply turn on your television's music channel, programming it to your choice of music style and letting it play in the background without your having to plan a playlist.

CHAPTER 14

Beauty and Spa

Beauty and spa treatment is one area where you don't want to go nuts with the freebies. It's your *perfect wedding day look* we're talking about, and a disastrous free hair dye at a beauty school can fry your hair right off your head. A coupon for a free tanning session at a sketchy tanning center that just popped up in a strip mall can spell disaster for your skin. And a free waxing—well, that just doesn't sound like a good idea *at all*.

When it comes to your wedding day beauty, just like your wedding gown, you're aiming for pleasant little add-ons that can boost your brilliance and shine. How you look and feel is way too important to risk in pursuit of a random freebie you know nothing about.

Besides fried hair and a scorched tan, there's another very important factor in this section—having the *experience* of being made up by a professional is part of the bridal dream. It's your celebrity moment, as talented pros transform you from morning-hair-ponytail-mess to magazine-cover goddess. For many brides, the moment the beauty treatments start, they forget about their prewedding stress and feel like a million bucks. Ten million, perhaps.

As I mention many times in this book, not all freebies are wise freebies. So let's walk beautifully through this chapter, spotting the *smart* freebie opportunities within your expert stylings and literally all around you.

The stylists you always go to *know* you. They know your hair's personality, such as what your cuticles do in the humid weather. Many have

What to Expect

IF YOU WIN BEAUTY TREATMENTS, DO YOUR RESEARCH

You're going to find a lot of opportunities to win free wedding day hairstyling, makeup application, even faux lash applications from beauty salons displaying at the bridal shows you attend. If you win their door prizes, scoring free wedding day treatments, remember that you have to put these experts—like every wedding expert—to the test. Visit their salon to see how they work. Do they have a real salon? Or does the pro travel with a suitcase of cosmetics and used brushes? Check for licenses and insurance—yes, you can ask to see those things. You're thinking about trusting your face, hair, skin, and nails to them—they'd better be legit. Ask friends if anyone has used their services, and if you get no insight, nor does your "gut-check" say this salon's the one for you, skip that freebie and talk instead to your regular salon's stylists, who know you, know your hair, know your skin, and are likely to give you a discount or some freebies.

files on what they've done during your visits—which highlight shade they use on you, which products are best for your hair, and more. "My stylist knows that I have been growing out my bangs for over a year to have the look I wanted on my wedding day," says Stacie, a bride-to-be. "And when I very stupidly used a coupon for a free makeover, the stylist chopped off a dry section of my bangs with those thinning scissors. Now, they flip out sideways and look terrible. I had to crawl back to my stylist, who I know was insulted and thought I was an idiot. There's no way I'm getting my long, straight bangs look for my wedding day."

Even if you have to pay a lot, consider it an investment to have the stylists who know everything about you be the ones who create your wedding look. Your own stylist might not be the Wedding Updo Specialist in the salon—many salons have their own in-house updo experts—but she will be right there to show the expert who is creating your style where you have a troublesome wave or to suggest a styling product that works with your hair's personality. It may not be free, but it'll be priceless when you look better than you ever hoped.

The Salon's Wedding Package

It's a rare beauty salon that doesn't have a special wedding package for brides to have their trial hair and makeup done, their wedding day hair and makeup, beauty works for the bridesmaids and moms, and perhaps even a champagne breakfast. These packages are specially designed by the salon owners, who know which options are the most popular, and are priced according to the salon's elite level of service.

As a freebie-hunter, you may see a list of *gratis* elements in that bridal package, such as a free mani/pedi for you with bookings of hair and makeup for three bridesmaids, or a free hair trial several months before the wedding. Free veil attachment. Free faux lash application. And so on. The greatest number of freebies exist with these platinum packages, but you do have it in your power to ask for a freebie or two even if you don't have that platinum package booked. If your wedding brings in six bridesmaids, the moms, and the flower girls, all paying for their own hair and makeup—if that's what you've arranged—or on your dime, you're an excellent source of income for the day. So ask if you can get a little reward.

Or, ask for some switches of *equal-value* products or services, such as a straightening for your one bridesmaid, instead of an updo, or makeup for everyone in place of mani/pedis. The girls can do their own nails

Here's What to Say

HOW TO ASK FOR BEAUTY FREEBIES

You: "Since we have so many people in our party, each getting hair, makeup, and nails, I was hoping that you'd agree to upgrade my makeup to airbrush, or grant me lash extensions." Most salon owners would be glad to do so and not offended that you asked. They *would* be offended if you tried to muscle them with, "Over at [other salon], they give the bride free *everything* when their bridesmaids and moms get their hair done. So . . ." The salon owner knows the place down the block is hurting for customers after a few bad Yelp reviews, which is why it is giving services away. Salon owners are more likely to say yes to an optimistic request, and far more likely to say no to an attempted manipulation, even if you say it sweetly.

earlier that morning, and just enjoy an airbrush makeup application at the salon.

Now, of course, many brides on a budget release their equally budget-conscious bridesmaids from having their hair, makeup, and nails done. They wouldn't ask their girls to pay for those services, nor can they pay for their girls to get them. If you're going solo to the salon, you may be far better off skipping the bridal package and just getting your hair and makeup done. There may be no freebies, but by virtue of paying only $100 for your own bridal beauty, rather than $300 for the group's sessions or the platinum package for all, you've just earned $200 worth of *free* someplace else in your budget.

Or, you can give your bridesmaids their wedding day beauty treatments as their thank-you gift. As one bridesmaid said, "Just having my hair done in a really pretty, romantic up-do was something I've always wanted. It was a great gift."

Getting Gorgeous

Now, we'll go step-by-step through each of the beauty services you wish to have for your wedding day. Some universal rules apply:

- You can ask your friends and family members to give you gift cards to your favorite beauty salon for your birthday, the holidays, graduation, or any event for which you will receive gifts within a year of the wedding. If ten people give you $25 gift cards, that's your entire bridal package for free.

- If you have a friend who is a professional beauty expert, ask her if she'll do your hair, makeup, or nails for your wedding day, as her wedding gift to you.

- If you have a friend, or even a teenage niece, who can wield a flat iron like nobody's business, perhaps she can polish the ponytail styles of your bridesmaids as her wedding gift to you—and perhaps yours as well.

- You *can* use beauty products you own on your wedding day look. Just practice creating the particular look you want—a kohl liner can do a demure daytime line or a smoky eye for evening. Remember, Her Royal Highness Catherine Duchess of Cambridge did her own wedding day makeup, so if your budget calls for DIY makeup or DIY styling gel for your hair, you're in great company.

HAIR

Many brides envision their beautiful wedding day hairstyle almost as often as they think about their wedding gown, and it's now a trend for brides to arrange for *two* hairstyle looks—one for the ceremony and one for the reception, and maybe a third for the after-party.

This is one of those topics where I'm warning you from going too far to save money. With everything you put into your wedding day look and your magical wedding scene, you really don't want to make your grand entrance to the sounds of trumpets and have everyone's eyes go right to your half-fallen hairstyle that's a bit greasy-looking because there's too much product in it. Or is purple-tinted because of a bad home dye job. That's what can happen to the DIY hair bride who tries to self-style or entrusts her tresses to a friend wielding a curling iron and a big pump bottle of shine gel.

What to Expect

IT'S ALL ABOUT A STYLE THAT HOLDS

An elaborate updo with lots of tendrils and complicated construction should really be created by a talented professional, for initial jaw-dropping style and *especially* for all-day and all-night hold. You want that pretty updo to last and last, through hours of dancing, on a hot and humid day. If you have your heart set on a gorgeous updo, make an appointment with a pro. And if this trial session is free, tip your hairstylist well. It's still time and effort she's spending on you, which should be rewarded.

You might choose to use your own hairstyle gear for your wedding day, but—and consider this fair warning, courtesy of dozens of brides who dished about those hair-updo spirals and lifting inserts that you find in beauty shops—only if you have mastered the art of twisting and if you're blessed with thicker hair that holds better.

But if you *haven't* used such gear before, and a friend offers to lend hers to you, you better practice, practice, practice. Otherwise, you risk a hairstyle that falls or shifts in a breeze or in the hot summer sun. Either way, experience or not, it's a risk.

Again, a pro can create your style and make it last, so it may be wiser for you to use these freebie hair gadgets at your rehearsal dinner or another event to get that budget break, and not risk a hair disaster on your wedding day, captured forever in your wedding photos and video.

Here are some smart freebies when it comes to your DIY hairstyle, for any wedding-related event:

- Watch online videos that help you create a sleek updo such as a chignon or a side braid. You'll find lots of these posted via links on your favorite bridal blogs and wedding websites. Wedding authorities often commission their own hair experts to shoot these instructional videos.

- Go sleek and smooth. A pulled-back ponytail, which you accent with fresh flowers or jeweled pins, looks elegant, polished, and either formal with lots of bling or an orchid, or informal if you leave it minimally adorned. Your bridesmaids, too, can wear slicked-back ponytails, or looser ponytails with some wave in them, and you all get to enjoy the budget break while looking fabulous on the wedding day.

If your wedding will take place on a beach, on a boat, or—this one escapes the caution of many brides—on a rooftop where winds may be much higher than on the ground, you'll likely be best-served by a ponytail

Real Stories

TAKE THE BREEZE INTO ACCOUNT FOR YOUR DIY 'DO

"I didn't even think about what the oceanfront wind was going to be like when I had my, and my bridesmaids', hair styled in romantic updos at a cost of over $300. At my beach ceremony, the wind whipped up so badly that everyone's hairstyle fell apart, and we had our hair blowing in our faces. . . . It was a disaster. We had to take out tons of bobby pins and brush out our hair right after the ceremony. It was a huge waste of money and I cried."—Melissa, recent bride from Akron

hairstyle or a pony with a curled-under back chignon that's been highly secured with pins.

The bottom line: When it comes to your hair, treat it with love—and as the frame to your face and a large and important element of your wedding day beauty. Trying to get it styled, dyed, cut, extended, or straightened for free could spell disaster. So this is one category that is often best left off of your freebie strategy list. You'll find lots of other freebies to make up for your smart financial investment here.

Look through bridal magazines to find stunning hairstyles—try libraries for free issues—and check out all of the free hairstyle galleries online at bridal sites, women's magazine sites, fashion magazine sites (they often round up the best hairstyle trends as well), and websites for bridal veils and tiaras. Great, free photos of hairstyles there.

And here are just some of the fabulous websites that feature free hairstyle how-to videos for your own DIY practice sessions:

- Beauty-and-the-Bath.com

- DIY-Weddings.com

- eHow.com

- HairstyleZone.com

- HerbalEssences.com

- Suave.com

- UpDoPrincess.com

- Womenshair.About.com

- YouTube.com has hundreds of them, posted by experienced hairstylists and celebrity hairstylists, including segments from talk shows in which celebrity stylists created DIY wedding day hair, and more. It's a gold mine of *free*.

Disaster!

SOME HAIR ITEMS SHOULDN'T BE BORROWED

I heard from a bride with a terrible story. She borrowed her friend's clip-in hair extensions for her wedding and found out too late that her friend's son came home with *head lice*, which infected everything in the friend's house, including her extensions. Yes, the bride got them, too, as did her fiancé.

MAKEUP

As mentioned earlier, Kate Middleton made headlines when she did her own wedding day look, and makeup artists everywhere thought she could have appeared a bit more dewy. But I think we can all agree that Kate looked pretty spectacular. She knows her best look, and she seemed like a glamorous version of herself.

So if you're planning to skip the professional makeup application, and skip the experience of having a pro create your best face look, as part of your freebie strategy, there are some smart steps you can take.

Watch those makeup application tutorials that the top bridal websites and blogs post, showing you how to do a pretty daytime eye. There are *so* many video tutorials out there. I found some wonderful ones at:

- BobbiBrownCosmetics.com—Get tips from the master herself, for *free.*

- eHow.com—Just type 'makeup tutorial' into the search box to find countless video segments from eHow itself, as well as cosmetics companies' videos.

- LOrealParisAcademy.com

- LittleMissMakeup.com—I particularly love the video tutorials on how to do liquid eyeliner and apply faux lashes.

- Maybelline.com—I admit, I almost fell over when I saw its video tutorials on sixty-four different trendy makeup looks, with its beauty pros sharing product choices, combinations, application tips, and more.

- Other cosmetics companies' websites

- TotalBeauty.com

- Websites for professional makeup artists

Share these video sites with your bridesmaids, so that they too can start trying out makeup application tutorials, giving them a wedding day freebie in the beauty department.

Speaking of departments, department store beauty zones are a hotbed of free makeup applications, lessons, makeovers, and product suggestions. You don't need an appointment. Just step into that intensely well-lit section of your favorite department store, or visit beauty stores like Sephora, and ask for some help with your wedding day eye look. The trained experts

Here's What to Say

HANDLING THAT AWKWARD MOMENT AT THE DEPARTMENT STORE COSMETICS COUNTER

I know, I have a hard time walking away from these free makeovers without buying a little something, especially if the makeup artist tells me about her new baby or the big course load she has in college. But here's how you do it: "Thanks so much for working on me. I really like the eye colors, but I want to take some time to live with it, see it in natural light, see how long it lasts. Give it a road test. What's your name? Okay, (name), thanks! If I decide to get these products, I'll come back here and ask for you specifically." This works like a charm and is far, far nicer than what most beauty counter workers hear. You haven't ripped off her time. You may very well decide to come back and buy the eye shadow shades. But for now, you've enjoyed the lessons, you know how to line your brows better than ever, and you know where you *might* get your wedding day makeup.

at these counters will be happy to show you different looks and try out different shades, and you *don't* have to buy everything the makeup artists present to you. Don't get sucked in by the hard sell. If you don't love it and don't have to have it, you can walk away buying nothing.

Next up are the free makeup samples, and they are everywhere. Go to the websites and Facebook pages of women's magazines and click on their Freebies tabs to get connected to all kinds of corporate-run product give-aways. The first five hundred to respond, providing your separate e-mail address where junk e-mails can go, can get a free Maybelline mascara and the like. I've seen some spectacular freebies listed at the following:

- AllYou.com

- BHG.com

- LHJ.com

- RealSimple.com

- SwagGrabber.com

Look in the Resources section for an extensive list of freebie sites, blogs, Facebook pages, Twitter feeds, and more, for fun and phenomenal cosmetics samples, and full-size freebie sends. Before you do, though, choose well-known brand-name products that meet vigorous safety standards. Using a free no-name product that may have been mixed in someone's garage and filled with bacteria is not a freebie. That's an eye infection waiting to happen.

NAILS

It's not just your wedding day mani/pedi that impacts your budget, it's all of the mani/pedis that you normally have, perhaps your weekly ritual of getting your beauty fix at your favorite salon. Here's a smart strategy that might just get you a free mani/pedi for your wedding day: Ask your salon if it has a "Buy Ten, Get One Free" plan. Some salons make it "Buy Five, Get One Free."

So many brides-to-be discover that their salon has such a plan, but they just never knew about it. So they sign up, get an old-fashioned punch card, or download the salon's app that is scanned each time they go, and along the way earn credit toward their free wedding mani/pedi. And if the salon doesn't have a freebie plan, talk to the owner to see if she'll establish one. The best marketing ideas come from customers, many company owners say. If their loyal clients are asking for it, they may just put it in place. Besides, it can't hurt to ask.

Again, your free mani/pedi might be a gift card from your sister or from a far-away best friend who can't attend the wedding and wants to give you something special for your big day, from your mom or stepmom . . . even from your groom.

Real Stories

A GROOM GIVES A PAMPERING PRESENT

"I couldn't get her diamond earrings, but I knew she'd really love getting months' worth of manicures and pedicures, and the special bridal manicure/pedicure package the day of the wedding, so that's what I gave her as a wedding gift way before the wedding. I love her, and I want her to have those pampering sessions that she deserves, so I packaged up a sizable dollar amount gift card and gave it to her as a surprise early wedding gift."—Daniel, groom from New York City

And of course, you can master the art of doing your own French manicure. If you don't have the knack for making that straight white line, it's time to practice. When I first started, I had thick lines, thin lines, pale lines, but now I create a French manicure that's every bit as good as some professional ones I've gotten. Better, at times. I just invested in a quality Sally Hansen French manicure duo kit, and gave it lots of time and practice.

There is no rule, of course, that you have to have a demure French manicure for your wedding day. Many brides paint their own nails pink or coral to coordinate with their flowers, their lipstick red to pop in their all-white regalia. Their pale blue toenail color can be their "Something Blue." And, of course, I highly recommend a clear topcoat to help keep your nail polish from chipping.

One thing to expect is nervous, shaky hands on the morning of your wedding, so if you plan to DIY your nails as a freebie strategy, have a backup person nearby who can take over and neatly paint your nails for you. Nerves can give your hands the jitters, which can create a streaky, edge-messy mani/pedi. A calmer friend can handle the task for you.

SKIN

You'll want your skin to be glowing, radiant, blemish-free, and gorgeous for your wedding day. Many brides choose to invest in prewedding facials to pamper and moisturize their skin, minimize pores, eliminate breakouts, and create that perfect complexion. Again, this is your face we're talking about, so don't trust it to random folks handing out coupons on the sidewalk. A free facial can make you break out more, or cause peeling, especially when unwisely planned too close to the wedding.

Talk to your salon's aesthetician about the ideal skin-care regimen for your face, and consider using some of the funds you've saved elsewhere to pay for these beauty treatments.

Don't forget your body as well. A qualified dermatologist will look at the bumps on the backs of your arms, the breakouts on your back, even the blemishes on your bottom that can be eliminated for a more confident teeny bikini during your honeymoon. Medical treatments are worth the investment, and since your skin is an organ essential to your health, don't risk health issues with free skin treatments or random skin products you've never heard of.

You likely have your favorite skin treatment products, such as moisturizers, bath gels, and other relaxing and pampering products that you use during your de-stressing spa nights. These can be added to your gift wish lists for those present-giving occasions. Check out Philosophy.com for an online gift wish list, and sign on to receive your favorite scents and products. Other beauty sites and stores also have gift registries and lists, as well, so check out the sites you visit often to shop for your skin and makeup products, and you may just discover—as so many busy brides do—that the sites do have free gift wish lists that you can use.

For bronzing and self-tanning, if you want to deepen your shade, go to a reputable beauty salon for a professional treatment. This isn't the time

Disaster!

DON'T DIY A FAUX-GLOW—ESPECIALLY NOW

Never plan to use a self-applied spray bronzer or airbrush foundation applicator right before your wedding. You saw that scene in the Jennifer Lopez movie *The Wedding Planner* in which a splotchy, orange bride sat there crying over her unwise choice to self-apply face tanner. Lemon juice and "scrub, scrub, scrub" aren't fun, and will leave your face raw and red for a very long time—if you can remove that product at all.

to risk your face and body with an amateur or DIY application. Or, make the most of your natural complexion and stay off of tanning beds, stay out of the sun, avoid bronzing pills, potions, powders, and all of the other browning products out there. Natural beauty is free.

Another part of healthy and beautiful skin is waxing treatments. Don't risk injury, infection, or one missing eyebrow by trying to wax yourself. If you're not experienced, you'll have more pain, uneven results, and, very often, ripped skin. That's not pretty. If you are experienced with wax strips and home waxing products, you might choose to take matters into your own hands, but be aware that accidents do happen, and a single tug can rip away skin, cause irritation, or produce an unwanted result, especially— *especially*—if you wax your own eyebrows.

Trust a qualified pro for your waxing treatments, and start going months before the wedding to get a feel for a waxing specialist's gentleness and expertise, as well as the quality of her waxing products. Go to an upscale salon, not the cheapest one in town, and specifically ask about the dangerous process of "double-dipping" that can spread disease. Hygiene in any waxing establishment is important, which is why it's advisable to spend more on a professional wax at a reputable salon.

Disaster!

ANOTHER DIY DON'T: WAXING YOUR OWN BROWS

Your eyebrows are *the* frame for your eyes. Beware of DIYing your eyebrow using wax with a strip and pulling off a portion over your eye; it's going to be incredibly stressful and obvious that you have a penciled-in section of brow.

PERFUME

When you smell lovely, you feel lovely. We hear about celebrities wearing their own signature, branded scents at their weddings, and we may be taken by the siren call of Vera Wang's perfume for our wedding day scent. Grooms say they love to give this as a wedding day gift to their brides, so if your groom is asking what he can give you, take him right to the department store to sniff some sample strips, and let him give you a freebie perfume you'll wear again and again, always thinking back to your wedding day each time you wear it. And so will he.

Relaxation

When you're relaxed, you look and feel better. It's not good to have so many stress hormones coursing through you. It affects your skin, your hair, your eyes, your energy level. Embarking upon a great, multitiered relaxation program is just as important as planning your fitness and weight loss program, if not more so.

Considering how important this category is, how greatly your relaxed frame of mind impacts every element of your wedding plans—such as avoiding making snap decisions about purchases because you're wiped out, or yelling at your groom because you're stressed out—you'll be happy to know there are a *ton* of free ways to get more relaxed.

MEDITATION

You could pay $100 to take meditation classes at your gym or yoga studio, only to find out that you can't let go while listening to the guy next to you breathe through his mouth. That six-week meditation course fee is nonrefundable, so that might turn out to be a loss.

Instead, accept that if you're not already a practiced meditator with a process that you know works, you're going to have to try several kinds of meditation to see what calms and quiets your mind and relaxes your body. And you don't have to buy books for that. There are plenty of sites with free MP3s and videos on a variety of meditation styles. I like the Gaiam Life Meditation Rooms (life.gaiam.com/gaiam-life-meditation-rooms). The upgraded, multi-feature Gaiam TV comes to you at $9.95 a month for additional programming, but these meditation videos are free. Each of the six themed "rooms" plays calming meditation music and a slide show of gorgeous images, or video. Choose from the Floral Room, Winter Room, Space Room, Forest Room, Water Room, or Zen Room for a different meditation experience day after day.

When your blood pressure rises after yet another terse chat with your future mother-in-law, just clicking on one of these meditation rooms that you've bookmarked can get your shoulders lowered, your breathing calmed, and the relaxation centers of your brain balanced again.

One audio meditation site is BlissTrips.com, where you can listen to free samples of guided imagery and soothing music, but the DVDs are for purchase. Still, it's a great mini-escape, and you can sign on for the site's Bliss Trip a Day e-mail that delivers a calming thought to your inbox each morning.

A great solution for those who can't sit still and count their breaths in traditional meditation, or get lost in a guided meditation that has you soaring over the tips of treetops, is a walking meditation. You're out there in nature, moving, but you're noticing the colors and striations in the leaves on trees, the little white rocks in the paved pathway, the arch of wildflowers growing alongside the road. Stepping outside and going for a walk is free, and it could be your newly discovered path to relaxation.

Here are some additional ways to get your free meditation fix:

- Check out YouTube.com and Hulu.com to find the most popular meditation videos and to connect with a meditation expert whose style works for you.

- Check out your phone's apps store for a free meditation app. There are lots of them out there.

- Check out iTunes's free meditation downloads.

- Look into swapping your DVDs for any meditation DVDs that other people have listed. At SwapaDVD.com, you can list all of the DVDs you want to recycle. By sending them in to barter, you get points, and with those points, you can choose meditation DVDs that other members send to you.

- Ask friends if they have any meditation DVDs they'd be willing to lend you.

- Ask for the gift of a meditation course during your birthday or holiday season. More people are giving "experience" gifts or gift cards to wellness and yoga centers, so your smart "this is what I'd like" mention could land you in a great class.

YOGA

All of the ideas in the meditation section count here as well—from the free yoga videos to the gift of yoga classes. But keep in mind that since you're moving your body and hitting poses your body might not be used to, many yoga experts prefer that beginners take actual classes where an instructor can guide their form and prevent them from strain or injury. So lean toward that in-person yoga class rather than a free DVD of a too-challenging yoga workout.

If you are an experienced yoga fanatic, re-energize your yoga practice if you've let it slip, and look at your cable television's health and wellness On Demand channel to view its free yoga workouts, which it rotates every few weeks to keep fitness fans inspired.

You'll also find free or low-priced yoga apps at your phone's app store, which could get you sun-saluting every day.

Real Stories

FREE RELAXATION CLASSES IN BEAUTIFUL PLACES

"My mom told me that the local arboretum announced free tai chi classes every Wednesday night at sunset, run by a tai chi master. I went, tried it, and loved it. The slow movements slowed down my thinking. It was so graceful, and the tai chi master was such a calming presence. And I love that it's *free.*"—Andrea, bride from Los Angeles

MASSAGES

Health studies show that massage is great for the body and mind, reducing stress chemicals and muscle tightness that can hurt your joints and cause inflammation in the body. When you're running tired, or angry, or stressed out, a great massage can make everything better.

Rather than pay $50 or more for an hourlong massage at some professional wellness centers, or sit in a germy massage chair at the mall, there's a free solution that just might be sitting next to you on the couch. Your fiancé. Propose a nightly hands-on massage tradition that could have him massaging your neck and shoulders, or your temples, or your arms and hands, and you then massaging his lower back, his feet, his shoulders, wherever he needs some un-kinking.

Physical contact with your love produces happy hormones called *oxytocin* as well, making you feel buoyant and bonded with your sweetie, so there are countless benefits to this free relaxation plan. Including this one . . .

Real Stories

HANDS-ON STRESS RELIEF FOR FREE

Cuddling, hand-holding, mind-blowing sex—with your fiancé, it's all free, and it's all going to de-stress you.

Workouts

Part of your prewedding planning might include getting in shape or losing some weight to feel better on your wedding day. Gym memberships can be expensive, and personal trainers or boot camps come at a price. So take a moment to review the *free* fitness options you have available to you, always paired to your fitness abilities. Walk the dog, walk with your fiancé, swim in your neighborhood pool, just turn on music and dance, pull that

Real Stories

GARAGE SALES ARE GOLD MINES FOR WORKOUT DVDS

"I went to a garage sale and saw that they had a pile of workout DVDs on sale for $1 each. I bought them all for $10, and considering that an exercise class at a gym costs $20, they became freebie workouts really quickly!"—Denise, bride from Orlando

fitness cycle out of the basement and get on it every night, work out to free fitness videos on your cable channel's On Demand station, borrow a friend's workout DVDs and hand weights, and follow free workouts on Hulu, for starters.

Part Three:
Freebies from Fashion Sources

Your gown, your veil, your tiara—plus what everyone else will wear—is one area that surprisingly has plenty of freebie opportunities. But you're not going to sell out by accepting freebies that leave you feeling hollow. Some dreams are worth every penny.

In this section, you'll learn not only how to get a free wedding gown and customize it to your liking, getting some of that "my dream gown" magic, you'll learn how to look for freebies surrounding your gown—the little additions to make it even more special, and of course, the all-important alterations.

You might choose to skip the gown section altogether, figuring you're racking up enough freebies in the rest of your planning to allow you a good splurge, and focus on getting other elements of your look for free.

And you're not alone. Most wedding experts I spoke to said their brides sought freebies and discounts in other areas but told them the gown was their Priority No. 1. No cost cutting allowed. They'll shop smart, but they're not going to sacrifice.

I couldn't agree more. Read on, and let's get you wedding wardrobe freebies that make you feel fabulous.

CHAPTER 15

Wedding Gowns and Accessories

Your wedding gown is *the* dream purchase for your day, and most brides would rather get *anything* else for free to make room in their budgets for their dream gowns. They just don't want to miss out on that fantasy experience of going to bridal salons, trying on gowns, and catching their breath when they step in front of the mirror wearing The One. The moms cry, and the bridesmaids tear up and tell you that you look amazing. And you may, for the first time, feel like a Real Bride.

So in this section, we're not going to cost you that fantasy. You're not going out to garage sales hoping to find a used Vera Wang hanging from someone's basketball net that you can wrangle for free when you buy a dozen other items. Yes, I *have* heard that story.

While our main goal is to get several things *around* the gown for free, there are a few ways that you can get a free gown. And what you do with it is up to you.

Many brides are lucky enough to be offered their mother's, sister's, or grandmother's perfectly preserved wedding gowns. They might choose to wear it as-is, like country superstar Miranda Lambert did at her wedding to Blake Shelton, delivering a sentimental personalization to a wedding dream. Or, they might decide to take that heirloom dress and have it redesigned to their own specifications. If Mom, grandma, or sis agrees, that dress can be torn to sections and completely remodeled with new sleeves,

Real Stories

START WITH MOM'S DRESS . . . AND HAVE IT REMADE

"I got my new gown by taking my mom's wedding gown—which I got for free—and having a seamstress redesign it for me. She took off the sleeves, reworked the bodice cut, shortened the length, and it looked like one of my favorite gown designers' styles when we were done with it! It cost me only $300 in alterations, but the dress itself was a very meaningful freebie!"—Elaine, bride from Chicago

a new train, or new beading on the bodice. Even though the custom alteration costs money, the gown itself is a freebie.

Some brides inherit a dress from a cousin or a friend, perhaps a dress that they bought for their own wedding, then changed their mind about. The friend couldn't return the dress, so she decided to give it to the bride. That would be better, she thinks, than having it sit in the closet. And perhaps that dress became a very generous wedding gift.

Or, the bride fought her way through a crowd of elbowing brides at one of those department store super sales, purchased three deeply discounted dresses, sold two, and thus the dress she kept was free. She might even have made a profit on the other two dresses.

You might have a friend who bought two dresses for her big day. She wore one at the ceremony, kept it on for an hour, then changed into a slinkier one for the reception. If you love her ceremony dress, she might agree to give it to you as her wedding gift. You can wear it as-is, or you can take it to a seamstress for the VIP alterations treatment, complete with your custom design of sleeves, bodice, new train, and additional bling.

Real Stories

SOMETIMES YOU'LL TURN DOWN A $5,000 FREE GOWN

"I was offered a gorgeous gown by my friend who canceled her wedding. We're talking an amazing, $5,000 gown with beautiful crystals, designer-name, the veil and tiara, everything. But I just couldn't do it. That gown represented a failed relationship and her broken heart. I felt it was bad luck, and I knew she'd be really sad to see me in it on my wedding day. My friends thought I was crazy to pass up a $5,000 freebie, but I just didn't want my dress to stir up all kinds of negative emotions on my big day."—Jasmine, bride from Washington, D.C.

An exciting way to snag a free wedding gown is to win it. You might be the grand prize winner at a bridal show, taking home a $3,000 credit to a chic bridal gown boutique, or you might win a designer gown giveaway on a bridal website or bridal blog. I'm finding that the prizes at bridal sites' Twitter parties and Facebook promotions are more valuable than ever, with $1,000 to $5,000 gown prizes becoming quite common. Keep your eyes open for these events, log in, click your entry, and you might win a free gown.

With the national average cost of a wedding dress, according to TheWeddingReport.com, at $1,697, your budget will certainly welcome at least a break on your gown price, if not a complete freebie.

Still, nothing beats that VIP visit to the bridal salon, where you try on dream dresses and share the experience with your ladies, so don't miss out on that. The experience of trying on dresses is free, after all, and you'll consider it priceless.

Altering a Wedding Dress

The greatest news in the wedding gown world is that many bridal gown salons offer free alterations. Considering that independent seamstresses can charge several hundred dollars for their time-consuming work, that's a fabulous freebie. Some department stores, too, offer free alterations by their pros, saving hundreds of dollars.

If you have a free dress you'd like to customize, in minor or major ways, find a quality professional by asking your wedding coordinator. He or she will know who's good in town, who's good but overpriced, and who reduced another of their brides to tears with a horrible, butchered dress. This is an important investment, so dedicate a good amount of time to finding a top-notch alterations expert.

Another way to customize a free heirloom dress is to have it dyed. Professionally. An expert seamstress has the top-tier fabric dyes matched

Real Stories

TAKING PIECES FROM DIFFERENT DRESSES

If you have two heirloom gowns to work with—say, your mother's and grandmother's—your seamstress can take the sleeves from one and the seed pearl beading from the other. So don't say no to any offer of a free dress, since your seamstress's eagle eye for details could point out that the pearls on your grandmother's dress are imported and very valuable. You might choose to put your mother's train on your grandmother's beaded dress, at a low cost.

to the type of fabric, creating a gorgeous effect. If you DIY'd your dye job, you could wind up with a splotchy finished product and a permanently stained bathtub. It's best to avoid the hassles and damage, and bring your freebie gown to a pro for coloring into the pastel shade, or even the bright hue, that you want.

If a pink dress is not for you, you may wish to personalize your free wedding dress a little more subtly. Sparkly appliqués bought from a reputable fabric store could be meticulously sewn on, or pearls, beads, or crystals can be hand-sewn on, in delicate or dramatic patterns. Send out word through your social networking circles that you're looking for crafters who have extra beads or crystals they'd be willing to sell or barter for, and you could very well wind up with hundreds of absolutely perfect beads to create your dream, sparkling bodice or hemwork.

And finally, a full-length dress can be altered down to a flirty, fun cocktail length if that's your wedding style, tied at the waist with a colored sash (free from a remnant store). You have the very same gown look that walked designers' runways for no cost beyond a basic alteration.

What to Expect

FREE GOWN ACCENTS FROM YOUR ALTERATIONS PRO

Alterations experts have a wonderful reputation for being quite generous with their huge collection of laces, beads, appliqués, and other gown accents. When your tailor or seamstress likes you, he or she will often throw in these pretty add-ons for free.

Your Rehearsal Dinner Dress

The best freebie is in your closet. Wear a little black or little white dress you already own—perhaps a vibrant dress you wore to a friend's wedding last season—just accessorized to look new. You'll save $60 to $200. Or you can trade in some of your old bridesmaid dresses on BridesmaidTrade .com, where you get credits to buy a new deeply discounted little black dress to wear to your soiree. With enough credits, it'll be close to free.

Lately, more brides are swapping party dresses with their friends, borrowing a pretty dress from, say, their maid of honor to wear to the rehearsal dinner and lending her a not-seen-on-her dress for one of her special occasions. Call this a legacy freebie-finder, since our grandmothers and great-grandmothers used to do this all the time with their friends.

Accessories

A gorgeous gown calls for gorgeous accessories, and you can get many for free.

One of my favorite tips is to sign onto the mailing lists for quality bridal salons, "like" their Facebook pages, sign up for their newsletters, and subscribe to their blogs. Many shops announce special sales and contests that could offer a free tiara or veil with your gown purchase. Just by being in their circle of brides, you could win a valuable accessory of your choice.

The borrow may be your chosen method of getting this freebie. It's an honor to any mom, sister, grandmother, aunt, bridesmaid, or friend when a bride wishes to borrow an accessory of hers, and some close women in your life may be willing to lend you their precious wedding day tiaras or their fine jewelry. Here's what you might be able to wear for free:

TIARAS AND HEADPIECES

Tiaras and headpieces are the most commonly lent-out items, since they're not often packaged up with the preserved gowns. Recent and long-ago

Here's What to Say

THE RIGHT WAY TO ASK FOR A TIARA-BORROW

You: "I just *loved* your wedding day tiara—it was so elegant and delicate. I'm on a really tight budget, and I'm seeing tiaras for over $600, so I wonder if you'd consider letting me borrow your tiara to wear on my wedding day. I'd consider your lending it to me to be your wedding gift, and I'll protect it with my life."

Friend: "Of course! I'm so honored!"

You: "Thank you! Considering that Queen Elizabeth lent her tiara to Kate Middleton, we're quite on trend here!"

brides keep these safe in hatboxes at the top of their closets. Brides are asking their moms and grandmothers for their "toppers" since yesteryear's tiara and headpiece artistry is so breathtaking, and they're also asking friends who married within the past five years, the past year, even *last week*. Don't count out asking very recent brides, since your gown and *you* will make that pretty tiara look entirely different. No one will spot it as a borrow.

If your friend or mom says yes, you just got a $600 freebie. And even if it's a $100 freebie, that's still a great gift.

What about a tiara you win through a bridal show or site giveaway? This is the safest of prizes, since the quality is right there in your hands. Don't forget that you can ask the vendor for permission to swap your prize tiara for a different design, of equal or lesser value, from his collection. Most vendors are happy to accommodate your request, and you get a style that's more *you*.

VEILS

Veils are quite often hermetically sealed with the dress, and since they're so fragile, some brides hesitate—or refuse—to lend them out. It's a piece they feel their future daughter would love to wear, something that doesn't count on a dress style or fit to be wearable.

One trend we're seeing is talented crafters *making* veils using a kit from craft stores, switching out their own high-quality netting or lace for the veil fabric provided in the kit. Remember, remnant stores will often let you take extra netting and veil materials off their hands if you ask while shopping for other goods. This could make your unique, gorgeous veil material entirely free. If a friend will DIY your veil as her gift to you, supply her with this material or let her know this ask-for-it secret at her favorite fabric or remnant shop. And yes, some friends *will* lend you their veils for free, a savings of more than $500 in some cases, in other cases way more than that. Brainstorm a list of possible veil-lenders, looking at friends' Facebook photos for a freebie-helping reminder of their veil styles.

If you're planning a cultural wedding with a specialty headpiece—say, for the ceremony—it too may be borrowed from relatives or friends.

Of course, there's always the option of not wearing a veil, headpiece, or tiara, and instead choosing to let your hairstyle—with a handful of beautiful, sparkling hair clips or fresh flowers—grab the spotlight.

JEWELRY

Of course, if your groom gives you a diamond necklace or earrings or your wished-for ruby pendant necklace for the wedding day, that's more than a freebie. That's a priceless tradition and keepsake you may hand down to your daughter someday.

A big trend among brides is to seek the "bauble borrow." If you wear your mom's, grandmother's, godmother's, aunt's, or sister's wedding-day diamond necklace and earrings, that's thousands of dollars in free jewelry.

And your much-loved ladies get the thrill of being a dazzling part of your wedding day look, with a sparkling piece from *their* wedding day look. Brides everywhere are catching their breath on the wedding day when they put on borrowed diamond or pearl bracelets, pave cuff bracelets, colored gemstone earrings, and other wedding day dazzlers.

Of course, it doesn't have to be their actual wedding day jewelry. Some ladies will not lend those precious pieces out, but they will let you look through their other fine jewelry to pick out a borrowable piece or ensemble, especially if you make this their wedding gift to you. A simple

Get It In Writing

NEVER BORROW JEWELRY WITHOUT A CONTRACT

It doesn't matter if it's from your mom, grandmother, sister, or friend, always put *something* in writing about the jewelry you're borrowing. Just a simple, "On May 16, 20___, I borrowed Grandma Tina's diamond dangle earrings (shown here)" Take and attach a photo of the earrings, preferably of Grandma Tina handing them to you. "I will return these earrings to Grandma Tina on May 31, the weekend after the wedding." You then get Grandma Tina's signature upon their return. It may seem silly in such a close relationship, but what if Grandma Tina has an unscrupulous son who wants to file an insurance claim on the "stolen" earrings or charge you with theft? Stranger things have happened. When it comes to valuable jewels, err on the side of overcaution and write up a legal agreement for the borrow and the return.

Disaster!

KEEP THAT JEWELRY SAFE!

Be sure that borrowed jewelry has secure clasps and that earring backings fit snugly. These are precious pieces to those who lent them, so you want to be sure nothing falls off of you and disappears. Agree to return their jewelry right at the end of the reception, so that no one has to worry about the safety of the pieces overnight.

diamond tennis bracelet or citrine sparkling necklace could be your free wedding day jewelry.

Don't forget that jewelry can also be borrowed for the engagement party and rehearsal dinner, so if your future mother-in-law offers her aquamarine earrings, tell her you'd be honored to wear them there.

If a friend makes jewelry as a hobby or a business, ask if she'd consider making your bridal necklace or earrings as her wedding gift to you. Keep in mind, though, that some materials such as freshwater pearls are quite pricy and her time is valuable. Still, she might think, "This is close to the $300 gift I'd give" and agree to make the piece for you, materials included.

It's not jewelry, per se, but a growing number of brides are adding jeweled belts to their ceremony and reception dresses. If a recently married friend wore one of these sparklers around her waist, she may be willing to lend it to you for your big day. This is often a $75 or more freebie.

Ask to borrow jeweled hair clips that you know your grandmother or mom has in her jewelry box or ones that a friend wore recently to her wedding. It's a stunning look to pin up your hair with these glittering pieces in place of a tiara and veil, or have them be your hair decor after you remove

That's Going to Cost You

ALWAYS OFFER TO PAY DIY CRAFTERS FOR THEIR MATERIALS

Don't offend your friend by asking her to make the pearl or gemstone jewelry for you without discussing payment for materials. It's presumptuous that she'd pay to buy the gems and have them shipped, so practice good etiquette in making the offer. She might say yes, if her funds are tight and if materials are pricy, so if you do need to pay for jewelry materials, consider her work on your custom piece to be the freebie.

your veil for the reception. Heirloom jeweled hair clips can often be worth more than $200, which makes this a fine freebie.

Wedding Rings

A quick note about wedding bands. Getting new ones is expensive, yes, but those are precious metals and the symbolism of the ring that stays on your hand every day for the rest of your life is even more precious. Unless you win designer wedding bands, in a major contest or as the spotlight couple in a morning talk show's free wedding, you'll need to save up to buy the rings you love.

There are some couples who use heirloom rings, having their great-grandmother's or father's wedding band refitted to fit the bride's or groom's hand, and there are those who take the stones from an heirloom band and simply buy a gorgeous new precious metal setting for them. That's several thousands of dollars saved right there.

What else might be free, courtesy of your jeweler?

- Engraving inside the band, up to a certain number of letters
- Cleanings and prong repair for life
- The gorgeous ring box
- Ring cleaning kits, including cloths and ring-soaking solution
- A crystal or silver ring holder to set on your bedside table

CHAPTER 16

Tuxedoes and Suits

Your groom wants to look his best on the wedding day, and have his groomsmen, ushers, and the fathers look dapper as well. They put a lot of thought into choosing a tuxedo or suit that not only fits a visual image for the formality and style of the wedding, but is also made well and looks like a high-end outfit. Menswear designers create tuxedoes and suits from the finest materials, and extreme care goes into designing the dimensions of the tux or suit so that it flatters the man wearing it.

This is one of the many categories for which I will warn you not to cheap out and accept the lowest price possible, since you don't want your groom walking around on the wedding day wearing a tux or suit that looks borrowed from someone else. Quality is key here, right down to expert tailoring, to show off your groom's hotness and make him feel like Ryan Reynolds on a red carpet on his big day.

Here are the national averages for tuxedo and suit expenses, according to several top wedding industry survey sources, including TheWeddingReport.com and the Association of Bridal Consultants:

- Cost to rent a tuxedo: $500

- Cost to buy a quality tuxedo: $500 to $1,800

- Cost to buy a suit: $284 in 2011, which is down 11 percent from 2010

That's Going to Cost You

FIND OUT THE CURRENT TUX AND SUIT EXPENSES NEAR YOU

Industry surveys are often dated, and prices vary by region. Check out the current reported averages in your area by filling in your zip code at CostOfWedding.com or at theweddingreport.com. With a good look at the amounts spent in your area, you have a baseline to help you configure your budget for this all-important investment.

- Cost for the accessories, such as a shirt, tie, and cuff links: $91 to $116

- Cost of alterations of a tux or suit: $30 to $100 (a figure I believe to be low)

Tuxedoes

The most commonly seen freebie for grooms occurs when a quality, respectable, long-standing tuxedo shop offers the groom *his* tuxedo for free, with the rental of the groomsmen's tuxes. That's the best-known perk, which many grooms who are in a financial position to do so hand to a father or to a best man who's short on funds. It's quite a gift, especially when the father is paying for a big chunk of the wedding or paying for the couple's honeymoon, or the best man is spending a lot to fly across country to be there for the wedding day.

Before you promise anyone a free tuxedo, talk to the tux shop about your plans to do so. Some tuxedo agencies inexplicably have a rule that only the groom can have the free tux. It's nontransferable. Check to make sure your tux shop isn't one of these inflexible establishments, and then extend the freebie to the great man on your list.

It's possible to get *two* free tuxes. Many tux shops have a standing policy to offer two freebies with an order of more than eight rentals, a smart business policy that motivates positive word-of-mouth. If that shop makes a groom happy with two freebies, he's going to refer it to his other engaged buddies. The shop wins, and the recipients of the two free tuxes also win.

Here's a little inside secret about the tuxedo industry: Some tuxedo brands encourage shop owners to rent their tuxes out, with a company-sanctioned free rental for the groom. When you walk into the tux shop, you might see a sign reading, "Choose (brand) tuxedoes and get two free

Here's What to Say

HOW TO ASK FOR AN EXTRA FREE TUX

Let's say the tux shop doesn't mention a Two Free Tuxes policy when your order of the groomsmen's, dads', and ring bearers' tuxes goes into the eight-plus zone. You could make some freebie magic for yourself when you say, *"Since we're placing a rental order for twelve tux ensembles, would you be amenable to granting us an extra free tux? I know my dad would be very grateful."* Short and sweet. And asked politely. You're also mentioning that you intend the free tux rental to go to the dad, which many tux shops like to hear. You're doing a kindness for a parent, which shows your giving spirit. It's a very subtle motivator, working better than if you didn't mention the recipient of the free tux.

rentals!" Now, this is only a great deal when the advertised brand is high quality. You don't want to stumble into a "you get what you pay for" moment when that particular brand is made of inferior materials, shoddy lining, and poor construction.

ADDITIONAL STRATEGIES

A great wedding coordinator will tell you which tux shop to go to and which to skip. Mention to your coordinator, or to your floral designer, that you're looking for a great tuxedo shop that offers a free tux for the groom, and they'll be more than happy to print you out a list of them or make a call right then to get you an appointment with their respected colleague.

As you know, some wedding vendors work in clique-like circles, so they may have a stack of "free tux rental" coupons for a tuxedo shop they work with—and here's why this can be a smart move: that cake baker isn't going to risk her professional reputation by partnering with a shady tux shop that doesn't offer 100 percent satisfaction guaranteed and high-quality tuxes. It would kill her business if she sent you to a friend with bad service. So ask your vendors whom they know, and—specifically—who rents out free tuxes to the groom.

Ask your engaged and recently married friends whom they rented their tuxes from, if they loved them, if they'd recommend them, and if that shop gave a free tux to the groom. I know, normally, it's considered impolite to ask what someone spent on a wedding purchase, but this is an acceptable question posed to a close friend or relative. They want to help you, and if they can say, "Yes! They gave us two! And the tailor came to the hotel to fix one of the guys' buttons!" you know you have a great recommendation to check out.

Don't forget that some people in your circle, not necessarily the recently engaged, travel in elite circles. They might attend charity galas, balls, and other black-tie events. So they might rent tuxedoes or own one of their own. Regardless, they know the best tux shops out there, and if

Here's What to Say

ASKING FOR A TUX RENTAL REFERRAL

You: "Uncle Frank, where do you get your tuxedoes? We're looking for a top-quality tux shop, and I thought you'd have connections to the best ones around here." No over-complimenting Uncle Frank. Just a simple request for a shop name that might lead to Uncle Frank making a call to "his guy" to get you a discount or a freebie.

they're *really* good customers or friends with the owner, they might make a call on your behalf to snag you the friends and family discount on your wedding tux rental. Some arrange for free tux rentals for you when they're really close with the proprietor.

Get on the mailing list at several tuxedo rental shops right away, far in advance of when you plan to shop for, try on, and book your tuxedoes. That task isn't done a year prior, so the longer you're on the VIP mailing lists, the better your chances of being notified of the shop's specials, "free tux" contests, or "free tux for the groom" or even "free accessories for everyone" promotions.

Also, "like" the shops on Facebook and follow them on Twitter. Many tux shops announce "flash sales" to their loyal fans, including "freebies for the groom" for a limited time, using a code they mention on their feeds. Some companies *only* run their contests and giveaways on their social networking sites, making that a big reason to click on them.

If you have engaged friends, you might earn several free tuxes or accessories if you refer them to the tuxedo shop you like and if they book their eight wedding tuxes there as well.

Disaster!

FREE TUXES FROM BRIDAL SHOW PRIZES

Never take the free tuxedo you won at a bridal show without first investing a lot of time and effort into researching the shop that awarded you the prize. While it's true that quality tuxedo shops display at bridal expos to get in front of brides and grooms, some less-than-stellar tux rental companies (some operating out of vans, not storefronts!) will put up a website and call themselves professionals. Don't tempt disaster by jumping on a freebie that's handed to you without first checking them out. And if they say, "No, you have to sign right now" at the bridal show, that's not a sign of a quality company. Walk away. You haven't won anything of value.

ACCESSORIES

Shirts, ties, vests, cummerbunds, cuff links, shoe rentals, even those black socks that you'll want to be uniform among your men. They all add up to the $91 to $116 average mentioned at the start of this chapter.

Sometimes, the tux shop will automatically throw in free accessories for the groom, and again, you can ask for that if they don't offer, when you have a large or pricy order. It might be your secondary request if the shop won't give you a free tux rental. *"Would you consider a free accessories package instead, then?"* could persuade a shop owner to grant you that, and perhaps make that a new, smart sales strategy for his store in the future.

If you've booked high-priced, top-quality tuxedoes for your men, the shop owner may very well throw in free accessories for everyone. Some shops will do so, wanting to form a relationship with you. After all, this tux will likely not be the only one your groom ever rents. From weddings to formal corporate events, return visits are likely. Shops also want you to tell your engaged friends or want to impress the engaged men within your bridal party. Throwing in free cuff links, or free shoe rentals, doesn't cost them much, if anything at all. And garnering goodwill among your entire circle is how tuxedo companies stay in business.

ALTERATIONS

For most quality tuxedo shops, alterations are free. Shop owners know that the grooms and their men are paying a lot to rent their top-of-the-line tuxedoes, and many consider charging $20 to $100 or more for altering to be a faux pas. *"I don't want to look like I'm not doing good business by having to charge for alterations,"* says one tuxedo shop owner. *"If I'm a successful company, I don't need to charge for that."* You want to work with someone like *that* guy. So make free alterations one of your top criteria when searching for the best tuxedo place. Tell your vendors that it's a priority for you, and

Disaster!

WEAR-YOUR-OWN IS NOT A GOOD IDEA

Don't attempt to save money by telling your men to wear their own black dress shoes or to skip the cuff links. You'd be surprised at the difference in shades of black shoes and at how intensely the men's different shoes stand out when they're all in matching tuxedoes. It will be way too obvious that you made a grave error in creating your own freebie. And missing cuff links? That just looks tacky.

ask your recently married or currently engaged friends what they found as far as free alterations.

Some couples limit their tux shop search to places within their own town, or one town over, and don't even look at great tuxedo places a few towns away. I advise widening your range of shop searching, since a great-priced shop with excellent customer service and free alterations may be worth the twenty-minute drive to get to it.

Suits

Your saving grace here is the two-for-one or even three-for-one sale at your favorite suit store or department store. So many suit shops are running these promotions to move their merchandise and attract men into their stores, that it's become a big trend among suit-wearing grooms to cash in on the twofer by getting a suit for the wedding free when they purchase a new suit for work.

I'm even hearing from helpful *fathers* who go to these two-suits-for-one sales with their adult sons—dad buys himself a suit and lets his son, the groom, take the freebie.

And of course, there's the "get me gift cards to Banana Republic for Christmas" tactic. The foresighted groom tells his bride and his parents that instead of getting him random gifts, he has a plan to finance his wedding day look with the gift cards he receives for the holidays, or for his birthday. With $250 in gift cards, he can get a suit and tie for the big day.

WHAT ABOUT A SUIT YOU OWN?

Can a groom wear a suit he already owns? That's debatable. The suit would have to be super-new, worn only once, with no signs of wear and tear. And even then, it doesn't give that new suit feel. Brides often complain that their grooms want to wear their own suits, which the brides object to because it's not special enough. If you plan to wear your own newish suit, be sure to crisp it up with a new shirt and new tie to be a standout, stylish groom.

Real Stories

TAKE ADVANTAGE OF TIE SALES
AND LAND MULTIPLE FREEBIES

"We saw an announcement for a buy-one-get-one-free tie sale at a department store, and they were brand-name designer ties, displayed in a range of fantastic colors. We bought three and got the other three for free, saving $180 for ties that really impressed. My groom gave them to his guys as their thank-you gift."—Ally, bride from New Jersey

The same goes for the khaki pants and white shirt worn to many barefoot beach weddings. Go for brand-new on both; don't risk having your groom look like one of the wedding coordinator's assistants in his worn-out, not-quite-white pre-owned shirt.

ACCESSORIES

Brides and grooms often give each other something special to wear on the wedding day, so for your groom's next birthday or holiday gift, give him the tie he'll wear on the wedding day. Use your favorite fashion coupon code site like RetailMeNot.com to land a big discount, or use a printed coupon at a department store to net the bargain and avoid shipping costs. His accessories given as a separate gift count as a wedding freebie.

CHAPTER 17

Bridesmaids', Moms', and Kids' Outfits

Let's make one thing clear: We're not aiming for free dresses for your bridesmaids and moms. It's important to look great and feel great in a dress you love, and for the wedding, that most often means a new dress of top quality. What we're aiming for here is some price breaks on the dress, and some freebies *around* the dress buy.

TheWeddingReport.com says that bridesmaids spend more than $1,400 from start to finish during their reign as bridesmaids, and moms might just be spending far, far more if they're helping to pay for the wedding or giving you a honeymoon as a gift. So they'll welcome freebie smarts for their dresses, shoes, and accessories.

Many dress freebies open to you, the bride, are also open to the ladies and kids around you. They too can get on the mailing lists for bridal shops to get advance notice of trunk sales and sample sales, with their VIP status earning them fabulous little freebies like sashes, belts, and gloves. And they too can shop in department stores that offer free alterations. In this section, we'll cover even more advice that you can share with the bridesmaids who are spending so much to be in your bridal party, throw you a shower and bachelorette party, and more.

As for your flower girls, their parents will love you for sharing inside freebie tips that can save on their pricy little party dresses and accessories.

Bridesmaids

Many bridesmaids say they're spending more than $300 on a dress and more than $60 on their shoes. If anyone needs a freebie, it's the bridesmaid who might be in several weddings this year. And let's start with the best freebie of all: *getting multiple wearings out of the dress they buy.* According to TheWeddingReport.com's recent bridesmaids' study, more than 65 percent of bridesmaids wear their dress two to five times, and 7 percent wear them more than *ten* times! So every wear after the wedding day becomes a big, gorgeous freebie. Think about it . . . that $120 bridesmaid dress worn five times = $24 per wearing, and you're not spending $75 to $100 or more on five new dresses!

DRESSES

The key to making the bridesmaid dress a smart buy (that becomes freebies each time it's worn) is to find a dress they'll want to wear again and again, not some $29 dress made of crappy fabric, that's falling apart and looking cheap. So, you can shop for that $120 dress, knowing the savings come FROM it.

Here are some top tips for finding bridesmaid dresses that may just be freebies very often in the future: Bridal shops now offer extensive collections of beautiful bridesmaid dresses, and they may offer a group discount to your bridesmaids if they order more than five, or if you order your gown from that shop.

If you'll look in department stores or in popular clothing stores like J Crew, Ann Taylor, and other shops that offer pretty or trendy dresses perfect for your wedding vision, make sure your bridesmaids know to shop with coupon codes via RetailMeNot.com and other savings sites.

There *is* a service called BridesmaidTrade.com that welcomes your bridesmaids to trade in their old bridesmaid dresses and even

What to Expect

WHEN CELEBRITIES MARRY, YOU COULD WIN

When a huge celebrity wedding is taking place, bridal sites and entertainment magazines like *People* go wild with wedding giveaways. So keep an extra close eye out for giveaways that benefit the bridesmaids as well as yourself.

non-bridesmaid cocktail dresses, formal dance gowns, sweet sixteen dresses, and other party frocks to get credits to shop for a new dress. It would be brilliant if you allowed your bridesmaids to each wear a little black dress of their choosing—not matching dresses from a designer's line—and each of your bridesmaids could get this new dress for free, or nearly free.

Bridal magazines have picked up on the fact that most brides have an average of four to five bridesmaids, and they're running contests *just* for the bridesmaids. Sweepstakes you'll find on the top bridal websites list prizes like: "free dresses for your bridesmaids, *and* a four-day, three-night girls' getaway to Cabo for your bachelorette party!" If you win—and with your four to five bridesmaids entering as well—everyone gets a free designer dress, shoes, and an amazing getaway with you.

The same happens at bridal shows, as more dress designers realize that bridesmaids attend as well. The shows offer fabulous door prizes of $1,000 gift cards to their bridesmaid dress line, which could outfit each of your ladies, with a little left over for accessories. Watch for these new promotions, especially as the wedding industry evolves during these trying economic times to capture the hearts of your bridesmaids regarding their future wedding purchases and their other formal dress needs. With each bride who comes in the door, these bridal shops could attract five new loyal customers.

Bridesmaid dress lines have popped up at retail stores like J Crew, Ann Taylor, and other popular brands as mentioned earlier, and here's another tip to improve your odds of catching a jaw-dropping sale or freebie: sign up for their mailing lists and follow them on Facebook and Twitter to get those fans-only contest and sale announcements. Many brands reward their followers with two-for-one offers, $500 shopping sprees, free shipping, and other fantastic freebie 'catches.'

Keep an eye on the calendar as well.

If your bridesmaids shop at a preholiday 75 percent sale, the savings add up to a free wedding-day shoes fund. And when they shop in-store or use RetailMeNot.com, they avoid those pricey shipping charges. Shop online only if your coupon code or the store offers free shipping, or—if possible, and better yet—go to the store itself and try on the dress. This strategy ensures a smart buy of a flattering dress and will also prevent you or your bridesmaids from having to ship a poorly fitting or poorly made dress back for a partial refund. Stores usually tack on $6.95 for return label use.

Find out when your state's tax-free shopping days are and what you may buy without sales tax, and let your bridesmaids know about these great offers; you might wish to shop for your own trousseau and other dresses as well. To find out when your state's tax-free shopping days are, just Google your state and 'tax-free weekend' plus the current year to find out the most up-to-date information.

Coupon queens get great deals and freebies, especially when they check out smart shopping sites. For instance, Pricegrabber.com will show you where a dress is currently on sale for the best price, and then you might be able to tack on an extra 40 percent off with a store coupon or code from RetailMeNot.com. Your bridesmaids can whip out their smart phones to grab deals via FourSquare and other apps, piling on the discounts until the dress is nearly free. And again, the money saved becomes a freebie somewhere else.

I'm also seeing bridesmaids cash in some of their credit card rewards points for a gift card to a dress store like Ann Taylor or a department store like Macy's. A $100 gift card can make an on-sale bridesmaid dress completely free. Share this gem with your ladies.

For their rehearsal dinner dresses, you also might suggest Bridesmaid Trade.com for them to consider if they'd like to wear a new dress to that event, or for any other event they have coming up. They'll love you for sharing the tip, even if it doesn't relate to your wedding. Bridesmaids can also wear a dress they already own to the rehearsal dinner. Enhance it with a new necklace or belt, and no one will know it's not new. One additional freebie dress strategy that's popular now is dress-swapping with a friend who wears your same size and has similar tastes.

As for alterations, which are so important for the bridesmaid's dress fit, bridal shops often provide free fittings, and many department stores do as well, even if you order the dress online. For instance, at Nordstrom, you can even bring in the packing slip for a dress you ordered online, and the store will alter it for free.

SHOES AND ACCESSORIES

Many brides give their bridesmaids a fantastic freebie break by saying, "Wear any style of strappy silver heels," or black strappies, or a nude-colored closed-toe shoe. Bridesmaids can then wear shoes they own, provided the shoes are in great shape and look new, or use a coupon or gift card to get a cute new pair they'll wear dozens of freebie-times in the future. Other freebies bridesmaids can enjoy: your thank-you gift of pretty bangles or a bracelet—free now and for future wears; a bridal shop's now popular offer to throw in a free sash or belt with a dress order; gift cards

Real Stories

TEENS HAVE TERRIFIC ACCESSORIES TO LEND

"I asked my sixteen-year-old niece if I could borrow a cute little rhinestone hair clip that she wore to her prom, and she said yes. It saved me $15, but I loved the way it looked, and she loved telling her friends that a bridesmaid came to her for a fashion borrow."—Liz, bridesmaid from Fresno

used to buy shoes, slimmers, stockings, or other accessories; and borrowed jeweled hair clips or headbands.

Moms

Moms get to cash in on the same freebies enjoyed by the brides and bridesmaids, including BridesmaidTrade.com, mailing list and Facebook sale announcements, coupon sites, credit card rewards, gift cards, accessorizing a dress they own for the rehearsal dinner, and more. Moms can also enter contests on bridal sites to win a new dress, since so many new contests are just for the mother of the bride and mother of the groom. Watch those Twitter announcements and bridal website contests, and sign on for any special newsletters these sites offer for advance notice of any Facebook or Twitter dress contests. *Bridal Guide* recently hosted a Twitter party featuring a company that markets plus-size dresses, and several lucky winners netted freebies and discounts from that hourlong chat. In addition to the sites that bridesmaids use for their dresses, where you may find a gown labeled as 'bridesmaid' that wows you, be sure to check local outlet shops that offer formal dresses and party dresses for 70 percent or more off. Visit

OutletBound.com to find top-name designers' outlet shops, and outlets for stores with Occasions dresses. You're at an advantage over bridesmaids, since you're buying just one dress, not looking for six coordinating or matching ones, and outlets can save you a fortune.

DIY DRESSES

Many moms and others may handle the economic crunch by having expert seamstresses reconstruct their already-owned dresses. They might have the sleeves removed, or sleeves put on, a full-length gown shortened, or beads sewn on, all at a fraction of the cost of a new dress.

Additionally, many crafty moms make their own dresses or use dress patterns to help them with dress redesigns. Here are some excellent sites for *free* sewing patterns:

- AmyButlerDesign.com

- BurdaStyle.com

- Butterick.McCall.com

- DIYFashion.About.com

- FreeNeedle.com

- M-Sewing.com

- Sewing.About.com

- Sewing.org

Or, as we're seeing more now, a talented friend, aunt, cousin, or relative who has extensive sewing experience can volunteer to make or redesign that dress as her wedding gift to the bride and groom. Yes, even a craft made for someone else can be called a wedding gift. Take great care, though, and don't invite such disasters as a busted zipper, a torn seam, or a fallen hem as happens often when an inexperienced DIYer takes to the sewing machine. This tip is only a golden one if you have someone in your circle who makes her own dresses or makes dresses for others you know.

Check out chapter 21 to consider if you'd like to barter your services with a talented seamstress who can help make mom a fabulous dress. And of course, all of the accessories tips for the bride and bridesmaids apply to moms, stepmoms, and grandmothers as well.

Kids' Outfits

These days, brides often allow their flower girls to wear little white party dresses they already own. Parents of the flower girls appreciate this price break, and with the addition of a colorful sash, these little princesses look as though they're wearing top designer dresses.

Crafty grandmothers can fashion the flower girl dresses themselves, especially for your wedding. This also benefits other brides and grooms who ask these special girls to be their flower girls, as the girls already have pretty white dresses, all ready for sashes to match their wedding colors. Those custom dresses courtesy of Grandma become freebies again and again.

And of course, there's the party dress hand-me-down from a cousin, that one-time-worn pastel pink dress that fits your little flower girl perfectly. Let the girl's parents know you'd be open to that option if it's something their family practices.

And parents will appreciate your letting them know about OutletBound.com as a smart source for kids' party dresses and accessories at big discounts, if they don't have a fitting party dress in their little girl's closet.

And yes, following kids' dress designers and flowergirl dress retailers on Facebook and Twitter will also alert you to special sales, freebies, and contests.

Real Stories

WHAT PARENTS OF THE FLOWER GIRLS LOVE TO HEAR

"It was the greatest day ever when the bride called to say, 'If you have a dress in mind, just let me know. My colors are pink and yellow, so if you can find something in either of those colors, or in white, just show it to me, and that will probably work out well.' I've spent $50 on some flower girl dresses for my daughter, and this was a great break for our budget. I called my sister to see if her daughter has a dress that could work, and she did."—Mary Ellen, mother of the flower girl, from Boston

Expert tip: Specify the color of shoes you'd like your flower girl to wear, so that she's wearing white shoes like you, not a white dress with black shoes. Again, she may already own her party shoes and little white socks.

Part Four:

Freebies from Family and Friends

Here's where you fine-tune your borrowing and bartering skills when it comes to your *friends and family.* You know that a friend-lent item for your wedding, or her DIY craft, can count as her wedding gift to you. Borrowing and giving often come easily between friends and close relatives—they love you and they want to help you plan the celebration of your dreams—but there are some important considerations so that these people remain close friends and family after the wedding!

What if the item you borrowed gets damaged or lost? What if you change your mind and don't want her tiara anymore? What if you're borrowing a *car?* Read on to find out the smart, safe planning details.

Don't be afraid to ask for borrows or for barters. It doesn't make you look cheap at all. In fact, it's a popular budget strategy in weddings today, and it flatters the person you're asking.

You love her style and want a little of it for your big day. She lends you her tiara or veil and then loves seeing you sparkle in it.

Borrowing also brings family history, culture, and tradition into your big day, adding extra personalized, sentimental touches. If Kate Middleton could wear a tiara owned by Queen Elizabeth II, you can borrow beautifully as well.

BORROW FOR MORE THAN JUST YOUR WEDDING DAY

Think beyond your big day to the many additional parties that might require some borrowed items. And think about how you can adapt that borrowed item for multiple uses. If you borrow a gorgeous punch bowl, for example, you can use it for the bridal shower *and* the rehearsal dinner.

Share this section with your parents or anyone who's hosting a bash for you. Tell them that borrowing is the new, big trend in planning parties on a budget and that you have smart "how to ask" scripts they can use when asking, too.

Here are some events around your wedding celebration to consider for your borrowing needs:

- Engagement party
- Bridesmaids' planning get-togethers
- Bridal showers
- Bachelorette party
- Rehearsal dinner
- Wedding morning breakfasts
- Wedding weekend events, such as a welcome cocktail party, casual cookout with friends, breakfast on your terrace, etc.
- After-party
- Morning-after breakfast
- Destination wedding needs

CHAPTER 18

Working Your Network

The people you know could be gateways to dozens and dozens of fabulous freebies. You're about to find out how to work your network *the right way* so that you can land high-quality items and help with your wedding plans without spending a dime.

You might think your first step would be to make a list of all the items you need to borrow, but that's actually the second step. Why? Because you never know what the people in your network of friends and family have to offer. It works much the same way as when you go to register for wedding gifts. You *think* you know all you need, the essentials like bedsheets and baking sheets, blenders and cappuccino makers—but then you make a left turn in the bedding section to discover amazing curtains and valances that you *have* to have on your list. You weren't thinking curtains and valances when you went to the store, but you discovered they were there. And you knew you could use them.

Each person you know is a door that opens to his or her stuff. And you never know what he or she has to offer that could be perfect for your parties. For instance, I'm looking in my own basement right now, and I have more than fifty lengths of little white holiday lights in my Christmas decorations bins. I'd be willing to lend those to a bride who asks for them, giving her a $500 freebie and a perfect lighting effect for her outdoor wedding.

Family and friends likely have lots of items that they may be able to lend you—all you have to do is ask.

Real Stories

YOUR FREEBIE REQUEST COULD BENEFIT THE LENDER, TOO

"When my niece called to ask if she could borrow some items from my daughter's belongings in our basement, that created the perfect opportunity for my daughter to come in and *finally* go through her boxes, get those items for her cousin, and send lots of other boxes out to the mission for charity sale. It was fabulous to get that long-awaited task done, and my niece received even more free items than she expected."—Maria, aunt of the bride, from Reno

This is where you start making a path toward countless fabulous finds, fun freebies that might add that perfect little something to a party's decor and might even inspire you to have a theme party during your wedding weekend.

You never know who has what.

Which is why you start off making a list of all the people you could ask for a borrow—and ask your mom and your bridesmaids to do the same.

Whom Do You Know?

It's truly a small world, and everyone you know might know someone with a $350 freebie. So here's where networking comes into play. And since networking is such an integral part in everyone's lives with Facebook, Twitter, Pinterest, and other social networking sites, it's never been easier for you to connect with six degrees of people willing to lend you things.

WHO'S IN YOUR CLOSEST INNER CIRCLE?

Your closest circle of friends and family are the ones who will lend you something really valuable, like a diamond necklace that's been in the family for ages, or their vacation home, or their antique car—the really elite stuff. They know you well, they know their borrowed item will be well cared for, and they're all too happy to help make your wedding dreams come true.

So start your go-to inner circle list with:

- Parents and stepparents

- Grandparents

- Siblings

- Your maid of honor and bridesmaids

- The groom's attendants

- Other close relatives

- Other close friends

Real Stories

YOUR NETWORK ALSO HAS A NETWORK

"I asked my mom to see if my aunt had any tables from the wedding she recently threw for my cousin, and my mom called back with the news that my aunt knows someone who has a portable light-up bar that we could borrow for the rehearsal dinner. It was so clubby and trendy, and everyone *loved* it. I looked it up, and if we rented a bar like that, it would have cost us $350."—Emma, recent bride from Chicago

Many brides and grooms say their closest work friends, with whom they spend most of their time, are also counted within their closest inner circle. These friends are well-connected with people in *other* companies and industries, and they might feel comfortable asking a favor for you.

WHO'S ON YOUR FACEBOOK PAGE?

It's an amazing thing about your social networking circles: Many people on your Facebook page—your childhood best friends you recently reconnected with, folks you know through your industry—are more willing than some of your closest friends to seek out something you're looking to borrow. Professional social networks are especially ripe with the sharing of resources, which becomes the golden return on all that time you spend updating your Facebook page.

The spiritual-minded among us would say, "You put your request out into the world, and what you're seeking will come to you." With Facebook

Disaster!

DON'T RISK YOUR GUEST LIST WITH PREMATURE REQUESTS

Don't ask for supplies too early in the planning process. You might have a list of people you plan to invite to your wedding, but as the planning goes along, you might have to cut some people from your list. Perhaps your in-laws need to invite twenty more people they didn't tell you about earlier, for instance. Wait a bit, let your bookings commence and your budget take shape, and then you can reach out to the definites on your guest list to see if anyone has that booster seat or bridal shower wishing well to lend you.

spreading your "Does anyone have a booster seat we can use at the rehearsal dinner for my niece?" request to your relatives, you might get a message two seconds later that your second cousin has one she can lend you.

So look through your list of Facebook friends to see who's there, and—this is important—make a special group list of those relatives and friends who are definitely invited to your wedding, so that you can message only them for your wedding supply needs or bartering wishes. It's bad manners to ask people who aren't invited to your wedding to let you use their things at a bash they *think* they'll get an invitation to. This special list keeps you etiquette-protected.

WHO'S PLANNED AN EVENT RECENTLY?

When thinking of people to borrow items from, go beyond the scope of those who have had weddings, although wedding hosts can top your list. Especially if you know they bought a great party tent for their backyard and spoke about using it for future family parties.

Think also about those in your network who recently hosted sweet sixteen parties, bar and bat mitzvahs, quinceañeras, a major milestone birthday or anniversary party, or a big bash that had amazing elements to it. If their party was within the last year, great. But don't limit yourself. Many who hosted bashes one, two, three, even five years ago may still have top-quality party items they could lend out.

One more smart source to consider: the person in your office who plans all the company parties. He or she undoubtedly has connections to people who lend great budget-saving party items, or perhaps she can connect you with a great-priced party pro with freebies in his package. And her referral gets her points with that pro for future company parties.

WHO'S GETTING MARRIED, TOO?

Join forces with your other engaged friends, and share all of your budget and freebie finds with each other. No one's competing, and fantastic

That's Going to Cost You

DON'T RISK YOUR JOB LOOKING FOR FREEBIES

Be sure that office friends and bosses are invited to your wedding before you start mining the corporate culture for freebies. You could actually get fired if the bosses hear that you're asking for corporate help with your wedding, or asking to use company furniture or other items as your freebies. So follow good company wedding protocol and ask for help only after asking for *permission* from the head honchos, who have received their Save-the-Dates.

freebies don't have to be kept a secret. It's good bride karma when you text your fellow bride-to-be to tell her about the item she's been seeking that *you* can lend her.

If you lend out something, your fellow brides might have an item in their own arsenal that can be a saving grace to you. Not only are you sharing information on freebies, you can also share information on discounts, sales, and your fabulous wedding vendors. If your fellow bride friend hires that floral designer and tells her you recommended her, you may just get a freebie or price cut from that grateful floral designer. It all works together.

WHOM DO YOUR PARENTS KNOW?

The parental network is a huge advantage to most brides and grooms these days. Parents have vast collections of contacts in many industries, sometimes people at the very top of companies who will be happy to give their dear friends (your parents) a generous discount on services, if not an outright freebie of great value.

You might not know that your dad's best buddy golfs with the owner of the best bakery in town, or that his old fraternity brother owns a winery where you can have your wedding or from which you can get cases for free.

Pretty soon, your mom remembers that your cousin had a wooden wishing well that her father made for her bridal shower or that your other cousin has a gorgeous chuppah she lent to another cousin. Once everyone's thinking, "What do we have access to?," the ideas come flowing at you.

It only happens when you ask your parents who's in their network—again, friends they plan to invite to the wedding—who can kick in some goodies for the wedding or the rehearsal dinner or party your parents are hosting.

Tell your parents that you're checking your network to see who has connections where, and ask that they do the same. If your parents think it's tacky to ask anyone to help fund a wedding, assure them that you're not

What to Expect

RESPECT PARENTS' COMFORT LEVELS

Some parents hate the idea of asking for a borrow, or any favor at all, from their friends and contacts. Parents I interviewed said they would never want their friends to think they're overextended in paying for the wedding or hurting financially in any way that requires them to ask for favors. That's understandable. Those parents who feel comfortable asking friends to borrow some chairs will do so, some parents who feel comfortable asking that bakery-owning friend for a break will do so, and the others will do what's most comfortable for them.

going to embarrass the family and that you'll only inquire about a borrow if the situation is 100 percent acceptable. Tell them what you learned, that many guests are lending items *as their wedding gift,* so it's actually become something that many people hope to be asked. But still, you'll be proper about it.

SPEAKING OF BEING PROPER

This is a *big* one: You have to ask your groom if he's okay with asking his side of the family if they feel comfortable lending anything for your wedding celebrations.

Just like parents, some grooms don't want to look as if they need handouts, and no matter how close you are to the family now, you might not know anything about the unwritten rule of your groom's family that you never put out a call to borrow things. Some families are like that. It can often be a cultural difference, or there's a deep wound from some past event in which Cousin Eddie asked everyone in the family to bring items to his daughter's wedding and he contributed nothing. Those kind of heinous manners live on in family lore, and no one wants to be the Cousin Eddie.

And you don't want to hurt your groom or your in-laws by making them the Cousin Eddie. This is one of those weird little foibles that you have to respect. Your groom gets a say in whether his family can be tapped for borrows. And who knows? Maybe his family has amazing amounts of fabulous party items like, oh, *$700* worth of light strings in the basement that take care of your outdoor lighting decor.

Once you get the green light from your groom, call his parents to ask if they might have any serving platters or extra chairs that you can borrow for the rehearsal dinner. Usually, you'll hear, *"Yes, do you need anything else?"* This is when you say, *"We'd love to hear about anything you have that you might like to let us borrow for the wedding events."* But don't stop there. Get specific. *"Since we're having a casual cookout during the wedding*

> ## Real Stories
>
> ### INVOLVE HIS SIDE IN YOUR SEARCH
>
> "My mother-in-law was the best resource in the world for getting borrowed items from her family, friends, colleagues, neighbors, and members of her professional associations. She said she was so happy to get my call about things we could possibly borrow, since she was hoping to have more opportunity to get involved in the wedding plans. She's really great at this, too!"—Mindy, recent bride from New Orleans

weekend, we're hoping to get some lawn games, too. Do you know anyone who would lend us their badminton net and racquets or their bocce ball set?" That lead gets your in-laws thinking.

TELL THE BRIDESMAIDS

Just a little extra tip about the bridesmaids: They have already been mentioned as being in your inner circle to ask for borrows for your wedding and other parties. But they can also use this borrowing strategy to help them with their own party plans, getting freebies instead of getting wiped out financially.

Suggest they chat among themselves, discussing their own networks, to see what they can borrow for events they're hosting in your honor. This is how the net gets spread. Pretty soon, your maid of honor is telling you that she has access to high-quality party tables from her office and that the boss lets everyone borrow them. Or your bridesmaid says she has a great margarita-making machine she would be willing to bring over for your wedding weekend pool party.

What to Expect

TELL BRIDESMAIDS TO THINK OUTSIDE OF THE BRIDAL SHOWER

When you mention the *other* events in addition to the shower, you inspire your bridesmaids to think about items they can lend for those styles of parties. That margarita maker won't work for the formal bridal shower at the country club, but it would be perfect for your swimming party and cookout. Once everyone starts brainstorming, the ideas flow, and the freebies come forth.

How to Find Out What They Have

This is the part that makes many brides nervous. Sure, you might know that your cousin has a portable bar that he lends out, but how do you find out what the others have in their basements? Unfortunately, you can't send out an e-mail saying, "Hey, I need the following two hundred things for my wedding, so just copy and paste this e-mail and star what you can lend to me." That would be tacky.

The solution is simple, and here is your script: *"Hey guys! We're in full swing with the wedding plans and having the time of our lives. We can't wait to share the big day with you. Right now, we're looking to save some on our budget, and we're asking our closest friends and relatives if you have any party-type items that we may be able to borrow. We're talking tables, platters, big coffee urns . . . anything that would work for several of our celebrations. So if you have anything that you may be willing to lend, please do shoot me an e-mail. We really appreciate your help, and we'll keep your items safe and get them right back to you. Thanks so much!"*

It's completely honest, to the point, and says first and foremost that you can't wait to share the big day with them. It's respectful and polite, using the key elements of etiquette, and leaves it up to your circle of loved ones to decide what—if anything—they can offer you.

Should you suggest a few items just to get their juices flowing? Sure, that's completely fine. The script above does just that. But keep your possibilities list on the small side, so that you don't kill the etiquette by sending a spreadsheet of what you're looking for. It sounds like a good idea from an efficiency standpoint, but you come dangerously close to crossing the line into tacky territory.

CHAPTER 19

How to Ask for a Borrow

Earlier in this book, you got smart scripts for asking your vendors to add some freebies to your order, and those contained wise wording to keep from insulting your wedding professionals. When you're approaching family and friends, you need to be extra careful with your phrasing.

If you ask the wrong person the wrong way at the wrong time, you might not just get a no, you might be immediately tweeted-about, with a "Can you believe she asked me for my *wedding veil?* Watch out, because she's coming at you next!" That *has* happened, a sad and regrettable consequence of asking someone who's not known for having a giving spirit, just because you wanted her veil. As a result, she's cut off your borrowing possibilities. Now other friends may avoid your calls, not wanting to be the one who said yes in your circle of friends. Petty? Yes. But that's why you need a smart plan *before* you start asking to borrow anything.

First, think about the person's proven penchant for lending or for doing favors. We all know which friends would do anything for us and which friends love us in a different way. They would drive you to the airport, but you're not getting their pashmina for the night. Everyone has his or her personal code, and lending out valuables might not be in it.

Be Prepared to Hear No

You should be prepared to hear no, and not take it personally. That's the number-one rule in approaching friends and family for a borrow.

Real Stories

SOME PEOPLE SAY NO AS A RULE

"I said no to my friend's requests to borrow my veil, since I know how fragile veils are, and I would have spent the whole ceremony worrying that she was going to snag it with her rings, or get it caught on something while she was dancing, or spill something on it. Yeah, I'm a worrier, but I just sensed a nightmare in that scenario, so I said I was sorry, but no, I'm not comfortable with lending out my veil. Not to anyone. If my sister asked, I'd say no."—Stacy, recent bride

It's not just "those friends" who may say no to your request for a borrow. Even your most giving-hearted friend or sister, or even your mom might turn you down, which can be immensely surprising and disappointing. It's just a reality. Different people have different levels of attachment to their wedding items, especially the Big Three: gown, veil, and tiara.

It's tough for friends and family to say no when they can sense your enthusiasm about borrowing their stylish wedding element. You might even get the "let me think about it and get back to you" response, which could mean good news in the end but may also mean that the person's trying to figure out how to say no without hurting you. It could go either way, depending on so many factors: Everyone has his or her own gut feeling to follow when getting such an unexpected question.

The Top Five Tips for Asking Smartly

- Ask for a borrow in-person if you can. Being there, being able to see their faces and discern that momentary flicker of discomfort, or worry in their eyes, is the best barometer of how people truly feel about lending you a valuable item—or even a not-so-valuable item like a platter. Asking via Skype also works if you communicate that way with this person. Asking by phone works, but it can be tricky to pick up signals in a person's response, like the slight pause or the hesitant stutter. Try to avoid asking for a borrow via e-mail since it's quite unlikely you can pick up on someone's true feelings in emotionless type and e-mail tones are often misconstrued anyway. And after you ask, maintain a conversation about other topics, so that

Here's What to Say

FLATTERY WILL GET YOU EVERYWHERE

You: "I was looking at the photos from your wedding, and I absolutely love your ring pillows! I've been all over the place—Etsy, the bridal website stores, the bridal salon—and I haven't seen any ring pillows that are quite so pretty."

Friend: "Thank you! We actually found them at a craft store and added the purple ribbon ourselves!"

You: "They're gorgeous. I didn't know you did the DIY thing on them."

Friend: "Easy as pie."

You: "They looked so upscale! Is there any way you'd consider letting us borrow one for our wedding? We can call that your wedding gift to us."

Friend: "Are you kidding? Of course! And wow, that's a really generous offer. I might just take you up on that!"

your visit or call is not just about what you want from her. I make this point often; it's that important.

- Tell her why you would like to borrow the item. *"I loved how your veil captured that authentic Spanish feel—the appliqués around the sides were so gorgeous!"* is way better than, *"Hey, can I borrow your veil? It's really pretty."* The person who may lend an important item to you wants to know that you love it for the same reasons she did.

- Tell her how long you'll have it. *"I would need to borrow it next Thursday for my first fitting, and then I'll have my mom give it back to you the morning after the wedding."* Or, *"I'm planning to wear it just for the ceremony, and then I'll take it off and switch to jeweled hair clips, so I'll be able to have it packed for you right after the ceremony by my wedding coordinator."* The friend may be thrilled to know her veil isn't going to have to survive your reception and the after-party.

- Offer to pick it up or pay for it to be sent. *"I'll be in town next weekend, so can I swing by on Saturday morning to see you and pick up the veil?"* Notice you said "to see you" first. Always, always put the relationship before the item you wish to borrow. If your friend lives far away and your borrow will require shipping, make it as easy for her as possible to get the veil to you. Offer to send her money for packing or shipping. It's a big Don't to expect her to take on the shipping task without your offer to compensate her.

- If she says yes, send her a handwritten thank-you note immediately. An e-mail will work as well, but it's always a touch nicer to take the extra steps to write out a heartfelt message in your own hand, on lovely stationery, elevating your message with the more formal delivery.

Disaster!

KEEP IT OFF SOCIAL MEDIA

Don't go on Facebook or Twitter to thank your friend for lending you her tiara, veil, or any other important item. It will open the door for naysayers—like her critical mother-in-law—to give her grief over lending out a particular item. And you don't want other people thinking she's a free lending store, asking her for other items from her gorgeous wedding. Keep this arrangement private between the two of you. The story of her veil, tiara, or ring pillows can be shared on the wedding day.

How to Ask in Different Situations

ASKING THE DEFINITELY GOING TO SAY YES PERSON

As you learned earlier in this book, moms aren't always a slam dunk when it comes to saying yes to a borrow request. Sometimes, they even flat out say no. So who falls into the "100 Percent Yes" category? That would be the person who, without your even asking, has already offered you the use of her vacation home on the beach as your wedding setting, or the friend who offered you her veil when you asked her to be a bridesmaid and has excitedly mentioned it twice since then. This person's a near guarantee, so asking her for a borrow is quite easy.

- **What to Say:** *"Aunt Viola, I'm just calling to see if it's still okay with you that Tad and I have our wedding at your gorgeous home on Spring Lake."* You're being respectful in asking again, before you start booking vendors who will be ringing her doorbell to take measurements.

- **What *Not* to Say:** *"You remember offering, right?"* Eeek, way to call Aunt Viola forgetful! This statement is just a fear of yours voicing itself.

ASKING FOR A VALUABLE, PERSONAL WEDDING ITEM

As mentioned earlier, some people may be very hesitant to lend out their own wedding veil, tiara, or gown. These are *their* precious items, and they might have a policy of not lending to anyone. Here are your scripts:

- **What to Say:** *"Just a shot in the dark here, but by any chance would you be willing to let me wear your gorgeous wedding tiara just for my ceremony? I'm always drooling over it when I see your Facebook photos from your wedding."* Now, stop talking and listen. This is the number one smart strategy of the polite request. This space of air here after your request is where you'll hear that awkward pause, the *ummms* and *uhhhs* of someone who isn't comfortable, at which point you back off with: *"I didn't mean to put you on the spot. Please don't feel bad about saying no. I know how important that tiara is to you, but I just had to take a chance."* If your friend is happy to be asked—flattered even—that's when you go into the details of the borrow, like when you'll pick it up, how you'll store it, that you'll wear it just for the ceremony and she can be there to unpin it, package it, and take possession of it.

- **What *Not* to Say:** *"Hey, I heard that you lent your tiara to your sister to wear at her wedding, and since you're one of my bridesmaids, I figured you'd be willing to let me borrow it, too!"* Don't get so excited there, manipulator. First, just because she lent her tiara to her sister

---

Disaster!

DON'T DROP THE B-WORD

Never wield your "I'm the Bride" scepter with friends and family to try to get that valuable borrow. The price is way too high. Make it a rule that you will never remind loved ones of their place in your bridal party in order to snag a steal.

---

doesn't mean she's automatically going to lend it to anyone else, and mentioning that she ever did is an obvious control ploy. What's worse is trying to muscle her into lending it to you because she's a bridesmaid. Obviously, she knows that she's your bridesmaid. The only reason you're saying that now is because you believe that role gives you some power, that she's indebted to lend you whatever you want because she's your bridesmaid. This is a bad judgment call, since your friend may feel obligated to lend it to you but be very unhappy about it. And unhappy bridesmaids don't exactly bend over backward to do other things for you, nor do they stay close to you after the wedding.

ASKING FOR A DECOR ITEM

Surprisingly, some people can be just as attached to their pedestal plates, planters, tea sets, and china soup tureens as they are to their wedding day veils and tiaras. It's one of those things that surprises brides, who often make the mistake of taking it personally or keeping track of this person's lending history. Pretty soon, these brides are fuming. Unfortunately, some people have a no-lending policy, and some people have an emotional attachment to what you're trying to borrow. *"I know it seems like just a*

$15 Crate and Barrel pedestal plate, but it's the last thing my mother gave me before she passed away. I don't even put it through the dishwasher." That's an example of why some people refuse to lend out decor items. But then again, some people do:

- **What to Say:** *"Diane, I noticed at your Thanksgiving dinner that you had this beautiful set of serving platters, the cobalt blue ones. I was wondering if you might agree to lend those three platters to us for my rehearsal dinner."* Pause, and listen to the reaction, to gauge if the topic is even still on the table (no pun intended). She might not know which blue plates you're talking about, since she has so many, including Delft china ones. You might have to say, *"The three oval ones with the light blue rims."* Diane might be receptive, asking you for more information. *"The rehearsal dinner will be at my parents' house, and we're doing a Tiffany blue theme. I thought your cobalt blue platters would be perfect for the serving table."*

- **What *Not* to Say:** *"Would it be possible for me to borrow those three blue serving platters? I mean, it's not like they're fine china or anything."* This may be a dramatic example of what not to say, but my point is this: Never minimize the value of something you're hoping to borrow. Insulting someone's taste level is not kind, nor is it a great motivator.

ASKING FOR A DIY PROJECT

This one defies the definition of a borrow, since you're asking someone to spend her time making something for your wedding. I include it here, since it's a great way to get a freebie. Remember, friends and family want to help you with the wedding, and when you make their DIY project their wedding gift to you, it turns into a huge freebie for them as well. Here's how to ask:

- **What to Say:** *"I noticed on your Facebook page that you're making adorable cupcakes for people. I wonder, if we call it your wedding gift to us, would you be willing to make cupcakes for the bridal shower?"* Stop and listen. The most obvious question will be, *"How many are we talking about?"* at which point you deliver the amount you have configured. Never ask before you have the count. It would be unfair to have a volunteer say yes to what she thinks is a manageable baking task, only to find out you want five hundred mini-cupcakes, each topped with an icing rose. With the number spelled out, this person can consider if this would be a great plan.

- **What *Not* to Say:** *"Considering that most people give about $500 for a wedding gift now, and I'm asking you to make about $75 worth of cupcakes, I'd say that's a pretty good deal, right?"* Ugh, how classless to throw numbers around. You're asking for a wedding borrow, not selling a used car. Granted, I wrote this to sound a little smarmy, and you'd never use that kind of selling tactic, but my point is this: Let *them* figure out what a sweet financial deal this is for them.

What to Expect

THE ONE OFFER YOU NEED TO MAKE

When you ask friends or relatives to make a DIY project for you, no matter how complicated, always offer to buy the supplies for them. The gift, then, is their time and effort, not the whole deal of supplies, time, and effort. True, this won't be an entirely free batch of favors or cupcakes for your bridal shower, but what's free is the time you save with someone else doing the crafting with love and care as their wedding gift to you.

ASKING TO USE SOMEONE'S CAR

If you have a friend who owns a classic or antique car, or a sleek, modern convertible, you might hope to make his car a part of your big day. Since the average amount spent on a limousine is $656, according to TheWeddingReport.com, borrowing a friend's or relative's fabulous car for the day turns into quite the fantastic freebie. You're not limited to five hours, nor are you charged a hefty price for overtime. It's a sensational deal if you have the opportunity to get a free ride.

- **What to Say:** *"Uncle Jeff, what would you say to our borrowing your convertible, with you as our driver, for our wedding day?"* Listen and learn. Is Uncle Jeff shooting his light beer through his nose at the audacity of what you're asking? Is he doubled over in laughter? Or is he open to hearing more? *"We've been talking about what kind of car we want to hire for our wedding day, and we both agree that your car is amazing. It's becoming a big trend now to have someone you know drive you from the ceremony to the reception in his convertible or classic car as a way to make a big entrance and also save hundreds of dollars."* Notice you haven't said specific figures. *"We'd consider this to be your wedding gift to us."* Uncle Jeff is now crunching numbers in his head. To bring his wife and two kids to your wedding means he'd feel obligated to give you a larger cash gift. In your region, that's about $400. He saves that money, and you save the $600 on a limo fee. You won't get the $400 cash gift, so that leaves you with $200 back in your pocket.

- **What *Not* to Say:** *"Uncle Jeff, we were hoping you'd let us use your car for our wedding day?"* Too vague. Scary. Fraught with the potential for damage to his car. You haven't specified that he would be driving it or that it would be used just for the two-mile ride from the ceremony to the reception. You have left too many things unsaid,

Put It In Writing

BORROWING A CAR MAKES A CONTRACT A MUST

When you're dealing with something as valuable as a car, and the safety of all the people riding in it, you have to make a solid agreement about the use of the car and all details about this borrow. Spell out the following in a written agreement:

• Exactly where and when you'll need the car to show up

• Who will be riding in the car at what time

• How many stops the car will make

• Who will pay for gas and tolls

• Who will pay for any damages to the car while in transit, as well as while in the reception site parking lot

• Who will be driving the car

• What the driver is required to wear (black, gray, navy, or tan suit, for instance)

• Where the car will be required to go (some people don't wish to drive these valuable cars in big city traffic or at the beach where salty air can affect their transmission or paint job)

- Insurance details (the owner's insurance policy should be in full effect, covering him during your wedding use)

- When you'll be done with the car

- If the car will be needed again to drive you back to the hotel

- If the car will be needed at the end of the night to transport anyone else (this is an important clause, since the owner will likely want a guarantee that he will *not* be chauffeuring your friends back to their hotel all night)

The car owner is really earning this one. After all, he or she has to stay sober during the reception if the car will be needed to take you to your hotel. Many brides and grooms consider this, but choose instead to hop on the hotel shuttle bus with the rest of the guests. Still, having a car at a wedding means the driver will have to stay sober or you will have to arrange for a designated driver. So add that into your agreement: Require the driver to be stone-cold sober at the time of driving you, and absolve yourself of responsibility should the driver choose to drink and drive later in the evening.

and Uncle Jeff's mind is going to spin all kinds of what-ifs about his "baby." This one's not likely to go well for you.

Always offer to pay for parking, garage fees, and especially having the car cleaned before and after the wedding. The owner may refuse to accept money from you, choosing instead to include those incidentals as part of his wedding gift to you. It's just considerate and much appreciated when you do offer.

ASKING TO USE SOMEONE'S HOME

That friend or relative who has the magazine-feature-quality house and gardens might agree to let you hold your wedding at his or her home. Some folks with the amazing estate and the gorgeous gardens, that view overlooking the cityscape or the ocean, make it a regular practice to host special family events in their home, and some have never been asked. Imagine what your cousins will think when you're the first ever to ask Aunt Jane and Uncle Max to host your engagement party, your rehearsal dinner, or your wedding at their manse. No one ever dreamed it was possible to *marry* there, and here you are doing just that.

Sometimes the owner of the home offers before you even ask. She's hosted the other cousins' bridal showers in her Tuscan-inspired gardens and, having no daughters of her own, takes great pride in being everyone's saving grace by opening her grounds for their special parties.

And sometimes it's a seasonal thing. Your godparents have a villa on the grounds of a famous ski resort, and your winter wedding would be perfectly placed in that gorgeous town with its celebrity sightings, its outdoor hot tubs, its gourmet restaurants and nightlife, and its gorgeous view of the mountains. Similarly, a shore house right on the ocean could be the ideal place for your summer wedding.

Asking to use someone's home for your wedding is asking for a big leap of faith. The person may not know the scale of your wedding, what will be staked into her pristine backyard, where her furniture will be shipped off to in order to make room for your cigar bar (that used to be her den). It requires careful decisions and planning, such as making sure the caterer's food trays will fit in the refrigerator or oven or else requiring the caterer to have her own separate food prep tent. It requires a lot of extra electricity use in the twenty-four hours before, during, and after the wedding. It requires a strong septic system that doesn't erupt on you. It requires a lot of thought, and is often best served with the wise mind of a wedding coordinator. In fact, assuring the homeowners that you're bringing in an experienced wedding coordinator can smooth your request.

- **What to Say:** *"Aunt Mary and Uncle Ken, we are planning a very small and very personalized wedding, and we would love it if the possibility existed that we could have our wedding at your house."* Stop, look, and listen. *"We were thinking of a ceremony in your gardens by the koi pond, with a portable trellis, and the reception in a tent over the tennis courts."* Aunt Mary and Uncle Ken are getting some valuable information here—you're not planning to wreck their lawn and gardens with tons of tenting. Just one tent, maybe two. Sounds reasonable. If they ask you to share more, you can explain that you always love being at their place, that it's like going to Italy, and that having your ceremony and reception in one place would be an enormous savings for you, making their home the perfect locale. Next, include in your request the important details: *"We're hiring a wedding coordinator who will make everything beautiful and see to it that your property is well protected at all times, and we'll pay for your professional cleaners to work their magic on your place both before and after the wedding."* Again, Mary and Ken are liking what they hear. You're showing extreme consideration for them, and protective instincts for their home.

What to Expect

THE WEDDING MIGHT SCARE THEM, BUT A SHOWER MIGHT NOT

Some people fear that a big event such as a wedding creates too much risk for their home, but they would open their home for a smaller, more controlled event. Imagine your gorgeous engagement party or bridal shower there, and imagine how happy your bridesmaids would be to avoid paying any site fees and get *this* stunning locale for the party they're throwing you. This home might also be the site of your welcome cocktail party for out-of-town guests upon their arrival the night before the wedding. Or the after-party, or the morning-after brunch buffet served al fresco on the terraces overlooking the pool and waterfalls. Look at every opportunity as a gift—a gift with free elements included.

Borrowing someone's home is a freebie in that it saves you a site fee and it doesn't come with rules such as a guaranteed minimum for your guest list, paying for the site's drinks menu, and more. You get more freedom to line up your own discounts and freebies courtesy of the vendors you hire, as well as other perks. But it does bring in additional expenses like that cleaning service; hiring catering staff and servers, bartenders, and valet parking attendants; and renting a large assortment of important items like a tent and guest tables. You'll also need to rent a generator large enough to handle the demands of your wedding *and* the household's power needs. These expenses do add up, so make room in your budget for them if you wish to ask a relative or a friend to use their home for any of your wedding events.

- **What *Not* to Say:** *"I'll clean it myself."* They may love you very much, but they're going to want professionals to come in and steam their carpets using top-quality equipment and solutions to get out any stains or footprints. Also, don't say anything along the lines of, *"And you get to show off your home to everyone!"* That's your braggadocio showing, which might turn them off. If they are the types to want to display their "good life" status to everyone, they don't need you to sell them that mind-set. They would be living by it. So let that one stay unspoken. Let them consider that perk quietly.

Put It In Writing

PROTECT YOURSELF, THE OWNER, AND THE HOUSE WITH AN INSURANCE RIDER

Whenever people open their home to a gathering, it's essential in this litigious age for them to contact their home insurance company to arrange for a rider, which is a special policy addition that covers them in case anyone falls on their property and gets injured, anything in their home is broken or stolen, or the property itself is damaged (such as in a kitchen fire caused by a caterer's assistant). These inexpensive riders prove to be a saving grace, giving the owner—and you—peace of mind, and saving you from lawsuits or expensive fixes. If you do get permission to use their home, make this protection-in-writing a must, and offer to pay for it.

ASKING FOR SOMETHING YOU CAN KEEP (AND CUT UP!)

This chapter may be all about the borrow, but as you saw in earlier chapters, sometimes you'll be able to acquire something from a friend or a relative and *not* have to give it back. It might be a formal dress or wedding gown you plan to redesign into your dream wedding style—including tearing off the sleeves or cutting a floor-length dress to cocktail-length—or a fantastic punch bowl your friends the newly married couple said you could keep because they got a new and better one as a shower gift.

How do you ask for these things? Directly. If you *know* that your friend isn't planning on preserving her gown and the dress has the "bones" to become a sleek, chic, stylish dress of your dreams, just say, "Hey, what would you think about giving me your dress as your wedding gift to us? I would take your wedding gown and have it redesigned by my seamstress into a whole new creation." Listen for the depth of her reaction. If she laughs, thinking you're kidding, there you have it. The request was deemed preposterous. So the answer is no.

As for the "you can keep it" item like the punch bowl, that's not something you can ask for. The lender has to be the one to say, "You know what? We just got a new punch bowl and we're short on storage space, so why don't you go ahead and take this one, then keep it when you're done?" To which you reply, "That would be fabulous. We could use it for three wedding events, not to mention family holidays in the future. Thank you!"

- **What *Not* to Say?** "Can I keep it?" is a line from a four-year-old. Unless it's an item for a craft, in which it's understood that you'll be changing the structure of that item and thus not able to return what you borrowed, you can't ask to keep any physical object you're hoping to borrow. It's always the realm of the lender to make the offer first.

CHAPTER 20

In Case of Disaster or Damage

No matter what you borrow, you have to take good care of it. When someone lends a table, she wants it back with all the legs working. When she lends her own wedding tiara, she wants it back with all the stones still in it. It's your responsibility to honor her trust in you by taking good care of what she's allowed you to borrow.

But what if the unforeseen occurs, such as your wedding tent springs a leak and soaks that borrowed table? What if you discover at the end of your wedding that a stone *is* missing from the tiara? Your first reaction will, of course, range somewhere from worry to terror—the latter being reserved for those special, sentimental items like the wedding tiara. Your friend may be devastated that her tiara is ruined.

Some items you'll have to repair, and some you'll have to replace. And the costs associated with those fixes can add up to a staggering amount. It becomes financial disaster for you, and a broken heart for them.

Yes, there's a big difference between the $30 table and the $300 tiara, but you need to treat each and every borrow as an extremely valuable item, no matter the dollar sign attached. Which is why it's time for what I call "useful paranoia." Normally, it's a bad habit to worry, *"What if this happens?"* all the time, but in the case of a borrow for your wedding, you actually *should* let that worry work for you. It gets you to think ahead of time of a plan for handling any disaster or damage that can occur.

That's Going to Cost You

ALWAYS CHECK OUT A BORROWED ITEM CAREFULLY

Not inspecting the borrowed item before you take it on, or at the moment you receive it, is going to set you up for stress, tension between you and the lender, and a financial hit. If your friend arrives with that tiara for you, take it out of the box, unwrap it, and explain, "I plan to guard this with my life, so I'm checking every inch of it out." Not that your friend *knows* a stone is missing from the tiara. She might not have seen those empty clasps with the gemstones gone when she wrapped it up after her wedding day. When you proactively take it out to inspect it, you can show her the missing stones so that you're not on the hook for them later. Skipping this step could get you billed to fix damage you didn't cause.

With anything you borrow, check it out in front of the person. Look it over, note any paint marks on the table, show her the scratch on the photo frame, point out the beading that's come a bit loose from the bridal handbag, anything you spot that has a mar. When you *do* find a little touch of damage, be good-natured, and ask for her permission to replace the glass in the frame or have your grandmother restitch those loose beads. Your friend will appreciate your offering to make the repair as part of your gratitude for the borrow.

What if the friend isn't there? If she's mailed you the handbag or the tiara—always via insured, trackable shipping—call her up immediately to tell her about the marks or the beading issues. Offer to take a photo and e-mail it to her. Lawyers will tell you that it's a smart preempt of a small claims court case to document any problems with received goods, and e-mailing a photo to the lender establishes a paper trail that can save your hide (and your wallet) later.

If the item is in perfect condition, it is smart to note that with the lender, as part of your thank-you note: "*Thank you so much for sending your wedding handbag. It's completely gorgeous.*" Why am I telling you to do this? Doesn't it seem as if I'm setting you up for that court battle later when the lender has a paper trail from *you* saying the purse was perfect? Because it's the right thing to do. If that handbag gets damaged, stained by lipstick or red wine, or snagged by your engagement ring, you're going to have it fixed or buy the lender a new one. She won't need that paper trail, because you're a decent person who's going to enjoy the good karma of taking responsibility and the gratitude of a lender who holds you in high regard.

Speaking of Responsibility

Every element of your wedding is extremely valuable. The things you buy, the things you borrow all become part of the magic that is Your Day. That's why I encourage you to think about insurance.

Put It In Writing

IT'S NOT PERSONAL, IT'S PROTECTION

Don't worry about offending a close relative or friend with this action. It's smarter to protect yourself than to leave yourself open to a battle and a lost relationship later. So be sure to get all proof of damage documented at Minute One.

Yes, insurance costs some money, but if disaster or damage occur, replacement or repair of those items may be *free*.

It all depends upon the terms of the insurance policy you have in place, and its fine print, including detailed lists of what's covered and what's not. Let's look at the three types of insurance that can save the day for you.

- *Wedding Insurance:* It's becoming more popular in these financially challenged times to protect the big investment of a wedding with a quality wedding insurance plan. Some plans will replace items damaged at the site of your reception. Some will pay big bucks if you have a health emergency and your wedding needs to be postponed. Some will pay for water damage if your reception hall is flooded. The possibilities are quite varied, and you need to be extremely familiar with what *is* included and what's *not* covered. For instance, some wedding insurance plans won't cover you for wedding wreckage caused by a snowstorm or other "acts of God." Some won't cover anything if your band doesn't show up. Each plan has its own rules, so spend a good amount of time and attention investigating wedding insurance that will cover as many potential hazards as possible. That "useful paranoia" comes into play here.

- *Wedding Site or Vendor Insurance.* It's a must for your wedding sites and vendors to have their own insurance plans. Quality vendors will have quality insurance coverage to cover any damages or disasters, which is why you always want to hire true, experienced professionals, not the cheapest guy in town who calls himself a wedding photographer simply because he got a great camera on eBay. When you interview and book your vendors, ask about their insurance policies and what's covered and not covered. In some instances, the item you borrow could be protected by the site's insurance—such as if a clumsy waiter broke your borrowed photo display easel. The site pays the $200 to replace it, not you.

- *Homeowners' Insurance.* This one is multipronged. If a generous loved one with a fabulous home and gardens allows you to hold your wedding at her place, her homeowners' insurance will often include coverage for damages and injury that occur on her property. As part of your early discussions with her about the use of her home, be sure to discuss the need for an extra insurance rider to cover your specific event. These riders often cover damage to furniture, to the grounds, and guest injury if someone falls on a walkway or trips on some tree roots in the yard. If emergency electrical work is needed, that might be covered, not paid for by you. Special event riders are great investments, for the homeowners' protection as well as your own.

That's Going to Cost You

CHECKING OUT THE COST OF AN INSURANCE RIDER

Before you offer to pay for this special event rider, ask how much it costs. If you're not an insurance salesperson yourself, you might vastly underestimate the cost and be stuck with a pricy bill. Your request about the cost stimulates a discussion between you and the homeowners: They may be happy to split the cost with you, or say it's part of their wedding gift to you. Or, they may expect you to foot the bill, which is understandable, given the value of their home and property. So save yourself by asking for financial information in advance.

The other part of homeowners' insurance is coverage at *your* place, where you will be storing all of those borrowed items. You want to be sure you're well insured in case of theft, fire, flood, or any other disaster. Make it a high priority: Protect those borrowed items anywhere they might be.

HERE'S WHAT I WILL DO . . .

When the person agrees to lend you something, even before you get it, talk about your plan to protect it. Let the person know that you'll keep her veil in your upstairs closet, not in your moist basement, and you'll keep it in the garment bag it comes in. Lenders love to know that you've thought about the protection of their valuable items ahead of time. Tables will be stored in the garage, covered by a padded tarp. Frames will be bubble-wrapped. You get the picture (no pun intended).

"I'll guard this item very well," you'll tell the lenders. *"But if something happens to it on the wedding day, I will definitely make every effort to fix it."* Lenders love to hear that, too. When you spell out exactly how you'll repair the item or replace it, you'll put the lender's mind at ease, especially when they're lending something of great value to them. Here are some possibilities to mention:

FOR DECOR ITEMS:

- Chips: *"If your serving bowl gets chipped when the staff at the reception site sets it out, or if guests using it are too rough with the serving utensils, I'll buy you a new one."*

- Tears: *"If the hem of your veil falls apart, I'll have a professional seamstress sew it up." "If your tablecloth gets a tear in it, I'll buy you a new one."*

- Stains: *"If your tablecloth gets stained, I'll take it right to the dry cleaner to have it expertly fixed. I won't make it worse by trying to bleach it myself."*

- Missing gemstones: *"If anything happens to the stones in your tiara, I'll pay to have it professionally fixed by a fabulous tiara designer my sister knows. She'll match the stone perfectly, and it'll be like new."*

FOR A LENT CAR:

This is a big one, and the lender's car insurance might cover any damages. Still, it's best to offer.

- Dents: *"If the car gets dented in the parking lot, I'll pay to have the dent professionally removed and the paint fixed. We know an excellent car detailer who took a big dent out of our car, and he does great work."* Keep in mind that this is a pricy, pricy fix, especially for some classic or antique cars whose paint brands and colors are rare.

- Fender benders: This, too, is huge for a quick fix, since bodywork can cost thousands of dollars. Again, the lenders' insurance might cover the repairs, but then their deductible may shoot up. Talk to the lenders about how they'd like you to work out this solution. As mentioned in an earlier chapter about borrowing a car, it's often smart to let the car owner drive you.

- Stains inside the car: *"If there are any stains inside the car, like from my lipstick or grass stains from my shoes, I'll pay to have a car cleaning service fix it up like new."*

FOR THE USE OF A HOME OR PROPERTY:

Those who agree to let you hold the wedding at their place are especially appreciative of your offers to handle any repairs needed, even if their insurance is all-inclusive coverage.

- Carpet damage: Offer to have their carpets professionally cleaned, if needed. It's shocking what can happen to a light-colored carpet when a large number of guests move between indoor and outdoor party spaces.

Real Stories

SOMETIMES YOU HAVE TO PAY FOR UNEXPECTED DAMAGES

"The people who let us use their home sent us a bill for new bathroom towels since they found stains on the ones on display in their bathrooms. We put out guest hand towels, but people still managed to use the fabric towels and mess them up. We had no choice, though. They sent us a bill for replacing the two stained towels, and we agreed to buy them new ones. Egyptian cotton, too. We cheered ourselves up by knowing we only spent $120 on the towels, instead of $10,000 on a country club setting."—Emily, recent bride from Detroit

- Stains: *"If there are any stains on your furniture, I'll hire an upholstery cleaning specialist to come in and fix it right up."*

- Broken items: This one comes with instructions for the lender. *"Before the wedding, please make sure you put away all of your breakable items like those crystal figurines on your mantel, your Faberge eggs on the breakfront, and other things that could get damaged."* You've warned them, and smartly sent that one in an e-mail for a paper trail, so you cut the odds of valuable items getting broken by nosy guests or bumping accidents. *"If anyone breaks anything, just let my dad know right then, and we'll get it fixed."* Why is Dad getting told? So that the homeowners have a plan in the moment and don't spend the entire celebration keeping that news inside.

- Damage to the lawn: Promise not to let delivery trucks drive on the lawn. Then add: *"And if there are any really bad divots from the tent or the seating, we'll pay to have your landscapers fix it."* One issue to keep in mind is that a tent in the backyard will almost always come with flooring tiles to create a level foundation and dance floor. That will compress the lender's lawn, even if it's just for a few hours. Flooring left overnight can cause pressure damage to a lawn and require some care by a landscaper, so be prepared to pay for that.

When Borrows Don't Fit Your Tastes

Here's one of those tricky situations that can crop up in wedding planning, requiring you to be diplomatic and kind: Let's say that a well-meaning aunt offered to let you borrow her silver serving platter for the reception, but when she brings it over, you think it's a little too ornate for your tastes. You saw the photos she sent, and at the time—okay, you admit it, this was a year ago—you were freshly engaged and just learning about realistic costs of weddings, and you would have accepted a Bengal tiger to walk you down the aisle if someone had offered.

What to Expect

WAIT, WHERE DID THE FREEBIES GO?

Right about now, you're probably wondering what happened to the *free* part of borrowing things or using someone's house or car. It's still there. You're getting these items for free. The expense of repairing anything in good faith are *maybes.* Still, it's wise to create a repairs fund in your wedding budget to cover you in case you do need to fix or replace anything borrowed. There's a space for Repairs and Replacement in the Budget Worksheet on page 261.

Now let's say that you told this sweet aunt that borrowing her silver platter means so much to you, that it's an important family heirloom, and you'll use it to display all the champagne flutes. But now you see that it's not just swirly and ornate, it has age spots that polishing won't get out.

Here's your rescue: *"Aunt Hilda, thank you so much for lending us your silver platter. We plan to use it to display the favors."*

Aunt Hilda's likely to be thrilled. That's quite an honor to have her platter as part of the wedding plans. And it's *very* likely that Hilda's not going to argue with you. It's doubtful she lives her life for that particular plan.

But if she *does* ask why you changed your mind, just say, *"We just love the way it looks with the favors. The edges of the platter are so ornate!"* And move on. You don't have to say that the platter's inside will be covered with a red velvet circle, on which the favors will sit.

If there's just no way that Aunt Hilda's platter can be a part of your day, you have to be honest. *"Oh, Aunt Hilda, we just took a look at it, and I'm so sorry to say that it doesn't match our serving pieces and platters, so we won't be able to use it."* And before she can argue: *"But thank you so much for offering to lend it to us. That was incredibly sweet of you, and that means the world to us."*

UM . . . I CHANGED MY MIND

Sometimes you agree to borrow something fabulous, you have it in your possession, you plan to use it, and then . . . you see a different style you fall in love with and have to have. Now, next to that masterpiece you discovered, the borrowed item just makes you sad.

It's quite scary to think about that conversation: *"Yeah, I know I told you I'd be honored to wear your tiara at my wedding, and you shipped it across the country—but I just bought one that's so much better."* I'm kidding with this, of course. You'll have to be so much more diplomatic.

Here's the Golden Rule: *If someone feels close enough to you to lend you her wedding tiara, she's close enough to you to hear the truth from you.*

Don't start off with *"Oh, this is so difficult to say . . . "* or *"You're going to kill me . . . "* Your friend will think you lost her tiara. Even though you'll certainly be nervous, those conversation-starters are manipulative and make you sound like a drama queen at the same time. Just say it: *"I was at my fitting today and didn't have your tiara with me. So I put a different one on, and I just got hit with it: This is The One. I don't want to hurt your feelings, since it was so amazing and wonderful of you to lend me your tiara, but I'm going to wear this new one. I just wanted you to know right away, so that I can get yours back to you safely."* Since your friend is that close to you, it's more than likely that she's decent enough to celebrate your falling in love with the tiara that's meant for you. She'll put you at ease right away, wanting you to have everything *you* desire for your big day.

But let's just say she's surprised in the moment and blurts out, *"But I told everyone you were going to wear my tiara."* This is normal and common. When people are surprised, the first words out of their mouths are often not the greatest ones to hear. *"I know, and I'm really sorry,"* is your response. *"I just don't want you to be surprised on the wedding day when I wear something else."* She'll likely realize that *that* would have been embarrassing for her. Not that all her friends would be able to tell the difference between her tiara and yours, but still she'd be hurt in the moment.

Reassure her again that you appreciate her kindness, and you love her tiara, but you love her more. That's what true friends love to hear.

"OH . . . NO . . . !" IF AN ITEM GETS LOST OR STOLEN

I wish it weren't so, but theft happens at some weddings. At chic banquet halls, quaint restaurants, oceanfront terraces, and in private homes, there are a *lot* of people going in and out of the property before, during, and after the wedding, and sometimes things go missing.

News reports often show security camera footage of sneaky little thieves slithering into a reception, going to the gift table, and walking out with a big wrapped box. And if a home is crawling with the setup crew and

> # Disaster!
>
> ## TELL YOUR LENDER TO INSURE FOR OUTSIDE THE HOME
>
> An important consideration about borrowed jewelry: The lender may have the piece insured, but *only within her own home* as part of her homeowners' insurance. It's a cold splash of water when the lender calls in her claim only to find out the diamond necklace isn't covered and replaceable because it was lent for an event taking place outside of the home.

delivery people, what's to stop a burglar from walking right in the front door carrying a box, only to walk out with a gift?

Insurance might help, but how do you prove that some sticky-fingered delivery person lifted your $500 veil? Without security cameras, the insurance company will likely deny your claim.

Whatever the situation, the fact remains: Something you borrowed is gone.

And as a responsible, decent person, it's up to you to replace it if you can.

LOST ITEMS

Not everything is stolen. I hear about borrowed jewelry that a drinking, dancing bride didn't notice fell off her neck or from her ears. In a panic, she summons her guests to get down on their hands and knees to search for the jewels, which is not fun when you're having a beach wedding. Someone's going to have to get the metal detector.

So, for jewelry, add an extra safety clasp to necklaces and bracelets, and be sure that your borrowed earrings have secure clasps on the backs, even if they're U-shaped danglers.

One new trend has put borrowed jewelry at risk: wearing one heirloom necklace for the ceremony and changing into another heirloom necklace, or a more dramatic new one, for the reception. If you plan to remove your borrowed jewelry, immediately put it in a jewelry case with a prewritten thank-you note and give it to the lender right there on the spot. Never hand her the necklace or earrings just on their own. Always package the jewelry in a pretty box or velvet bag so the lender can tuck it away and protect it.

As for the bridal suite where the bridesmaids leave their purses and other items? That can be a thief's first stop, so ask your site manager if she has a safe in which everyone can store his or her valuables. Those borrowed jewels go in the safe, where you'll retrieve them later.

Another category of lost items is borrowed goods that mistakenly get returned to, or picked up by, the rental agency. When you realize your borrowed tables are gone, you have to go to the rental company and look through the warehouse to find your goods. When silver sets and platters mistakenly go back, the rental agency will often recognize that the supplies

Real Stories

A SMART WAY TO KEEP THAT NECKLACE SAFE

"We told the lender that I'd be wearing her necklace for the ceremony only, and she decided to put it on for the reception, to keep it safe. It wasn't one of those huge, diamond-dripping necklaces she'd look overdone in. It was a subtle little pendant necklace, and she felt comfortable having it on, instead of leaving it in her purse, which was going to be at the table while she was dancing."—Anne, recent bride from Maine

Disaster!

THE ALL-TIME WORST THING TO SAY
IF YOU LOSE AN ITEM

What *not* to say when breaking the news? *"It is what it is."* Even if you mean to comfort the person, that phrase makes you sound disconnected from the gravity of the loss, as if you don't feel bad about losing the item and you're telling the other person to "get over it." Also not the best choice of words.

aren't its own and call you, but a busy agency may not even look at the shipments that just came into the unloading bays. It will scan your bar codes and count the stemware later.

So whether an item is lost or stolen, it's up to you to figure out how to replace it. So as not to panic your lenders, wait to inform them until you've searched high and low. Check every box. When reception halls pack up your favors, photo frames, and other take-homes, you may find that cake topper in a box marked "wedding favors." It's happened countless times. No need to worry the lender before you've done a thorough search.

Now if the item is truly gone, it's time to call the lender and apologize, offering to make every effort to fix the situation. This is brutal if it's a cherished item from her wedding or a family heirloom. Still, you'll work with the lender to figure out a replacement or reimbursement plan. Expect tears, expect anger, expect a lashing out in some cases. A lost treasure is a true heartbreak that no amount of money can fix.

In chapter 22, you'll see smart phrasing for making a rock-solid borrowing-and-returning-or-replacing agreement that could prevent this loss from escalating into a monumental disaster of epic proportions.

CHAPTER 21

Bartering for Wedding Freebies

Bartering has been around for ages—it's how many transactions got done in ancient days: You tend to my crops, I'll tend to your sheep. Now, instead of crops and sheep, we're talking graphic design services and kickboxing classes.

Many brides and grooms offer their talents and skills in exchange for items and services they need for their weddings, and they get valuable freebies in the process.

It works in one of two ways:

1. Bartering with people you know.

2. Bartering with people you don't know.

Sounds simple, right? But the process for each is quite different, although the rules are the same: You deliver what you promise, they deliver what they promise. Everyone is happy with his or her freebies, saving thousands of dollars each.

Before we get into the process of bartering, let's see what you have to offer.

Here's What I Can Do

Here we'll go category by category to help you jot down what you can provide as your part of a good barter:

- *Professional Skills:* If you're a graphic designer by trade, you can offer your work on a company's website, brochure design, direct e-mail layouts, or logos. If you're a day-care worker, you can provide babysitting. If you're a musician, you can provide music lessons for kids. And so on.

- *Nonprofessional Skills:* You're not a professional, but you can design a great Twitter page with custom graphics or you can design a WordPress blog that stands out. Professionals and those just starting in a new career would love to get those strong branding items for free, in exchange for something you need.

- *What's in Your Basement?:* It's a form of recycling if you have all of your old bikes in the basement, and you see that someone is looking to trade his carpentry skills for bikes for his kids. That person could build you a trellis to get married under for free. Look at the items you have to send out into barter world. Especially in demand? Craft

What to Expect

YOU'LL NEED A LICENSE FOR KID-RELATED BARTERS

On bartering websites, you'll see a lot of requests for kids' lessons in music, art, sports, dance, and other activities that parents want to provide for their kids but find too expensive. These good parents then put up their skills in trade. Keep in mind you do need to have a license to teach children, so find out your states' requirements for permits and permissions before entering into any barter agreement related to kids. This is a big must to protect yourself legally.

supplies. So if you went wild at the craft store a few years ago, buying up beads and jewelry-making supplies, but never took a liking to the hobby, you can offer those items as your side of a smart barter.

To help you figure out what you can barter, answer these questions:

1. What are you good at?

2. What would you enjoy working on, according to someone else's designs and specifications?

3. What do you have time to work on and deliver? This is important. If you offer to be a babysitter, do you have the time on weeknights and weekends to deliver on that deal?

4. What are you legally able to deliver? No matter how great you are at baking cakes, you have to have a license and insurance to do so, according to your state's laws. So stay away from any food-based bartering because it's just too complicated, requiring lots of insurance, inspections, and legal protection; you don't want anyone suing you over alleged food poisoning.

5. What is your skill or talent worth? It's smart to know what the per-hour pay is for your skill on the market so that you can make a fair barter. Look at Salary.com to see what graphic designers make, and do the math to see what a week's worth of work would amount to. Price yourself fairly but realistically, and not too low or you'll be resentful of the work you need to deliver at the value you placed on it. If you're working your butt off for too low a price, you can call that a loss. Another reason to know the fair market value of what you give and receive is the most important element of this entire thing—the IRS taxes on bartering. We'll get to that later in this chapter.

Real Stories

GROOMS HAVE BARTERING SKILLS, TOO

"Don't forget the groom. I asked my fiancé what he might be able to offer up in barter, and he suggested that he could offer guitar lessons, in the child's home, with the parent present, to avoid any hassles. That became so popular that he racked up a ton of barters and got us a lot of great free stuff for our new house that we would have had to spend money on. Things like the removal of a tree stump, some electrical work by a licensed electrician, some drywall installation in our basement, things that saved us a lot of money that we then put into our honeymoon."—Celeste, recent bride from Columbus

Expert Tip: If you're going to teach kids anything, make sure the parents are there the whole time, and make sure it's a safe activity, not skateboarding tricks or anything that can injure a child.

Here's What You Can Get

You'll see all kinds of things on bartering websites, from handyman repair services to tax advice from CPAs looking to score a new game system for their kids, painting services, housecleaning, pet walking and pet sitting, website SEO consultations to help a business get a stronger online presence, free haircuts, massages by professional massage therapists, and so on.

You'll also see services classified in the wedding industry, like professional photography, but I advise you to skip those when the offers come from vendors you don't know personally. Countless reports from professional wedding associations and wedding industry watchdog groups show that beginners and nonprofessionals are calling themselves wedding photographers without any training or connections to quality photo development labs, and are selling themselves in the barter system to work that priceless wedding day. The result is often disaster. Again, this book aims to get you *wise* freebies, not risky or disastrous ones. So, when bartering with strangers, stick to non-wedding industry barters, and keep your wedding safe.

If, however, you have a friend who *is* a professional wedding photographer, with memberships, awards, and a great portfolio, there's no reason not to barter with this friend for your wedding day photography, in exchange for your fiancé's last-season game system and more than fifty games, with his permission, of course. The warning above is meant for the bartering websites, where you'll be dealing with strangers.

This brings us back to option number one: bartering with people you know. We've covered this often in the previous chapters, but I bring it to you again to get you to revisit the idea with a fresh mind.

Disaster!

NEVER LET A STRANGER IN

We live in a world that demands caution. Be very careful about arranging a barter that has a stranger coming into your home to perform electrical work or other services. It would be a true disaster if you happened to connect with a criminal, rather than an electrician. Many barter system enthusiasts make it their personal rule to exchange only in goods that may be left outside their home or delivered to their place of business. Always proceed with great caution, even if you think you're being paranoid.

Some people prefer to barter only with friends, family, and neighbors they know and trust. For one reason, they know the person's work. They can simply visit his home to see his artwork, or see the friend's classic car that will be exchanged for interior design advice. In many cases it's just easier, and, for some, it gives them peace of mind. People they know will deliver quality work because they care about them.

That's the hope, at least. Sometimes you run into the opposite problem: Someone who loves you offers to make your wedding programs, but this person is not as talented as she thinks she is. So be sure to treat people you know just like the wedding vendors you checked out and *then* hired. Ask to see a friend's work before you say yes.

Here's a sample script for you:

"Do you have any wedding programs you've done that I can see? Or can you send over a demo? (Fiancé) really wants to be involved in all of the plans, so I'd love to be able to show him some of your work."

That's right, you put it on the groom. It's a fair truth. Grooms do want to be involved, and that's much more diplomatic than saying, *"I'm not sure if you have the talent to make the kind of programs I want."*

Now what happens if you don't like the samples she sends? That's a tough spot, since you don't want to make the groom the bad guy, especially if he had no involvement in this decision. Just say, *"Thanks so much for showing these to me. They're so lovely, but I just stumbled upon a design I absolutely love, perfect for our theme and exactly what we had in mind, so we're going to go with that. Let's talk, though, about something else you can design."*

That keeps the barter plan in place and her feelings from being hurt. Maybe she can make the itineraries for the guest welcome baskets instead.

When it comes to bartering with friends, be sure you love what they're willing to give you.

Now, with those warnings behind you, think about the kinds of things you might like to get through bartering, and keep in mind that you can get an item in exchange for a service, and vice versa. For instance,

Disaster!

DON'T BARTER OFF OF A PHOTO

Always ask to see a sample of the item mailed to you, not just a photo of a favor or a craft your friend is willing to make as her barter. Since favors are items guests will hold in-hand, every element of them has to be perfect. Anytime a guest will have a sensory experience with something—whether it's taste or touch—that item had better be fabulous. It would be a disaster if you saw a grainy little photo of a heart-shaped box filled with candies as your friend's barter offering, and in real life the boxes were cheap-looking balsa wood and the candies were poor quality. Use your own sensory experiences to test out a friend's DIY plan, even if that means going to the craft store with her to look at little wood boxes and to the candy store to pick out yummy chocolates.

you might be able to get a pretty pink aisle runner in exchange for your talent in writing some articles for the aisle runner artisan's website. Or, you might be able to get a night at a cute bed-and-breakfast nearby as a romantic getaway with your groom in exchange for a day of your work as a professional organizer.

Here are some *wedding-specific* items that other brides have gotten for free through bartering services:

- Trellis or chuppah

- Aisle runner

- Rentals of tables and chairs

- Tent rental

- Lighting services for an outdoor wedding

- Fabric for tablecloths and table runners

- Photo enlargements for display of the couple's photos

- Personal wedding website design

- Bridal shower invitation design and production

- Wishing well

- Prewedding mani/pedis

- Boot camp or personal trainer sessions

- Home cleaning for at-home parties

Inspired? Use this list, and Worksheet No. 5 at the end of this book, to develop your wish list of items and services you might find through bartering.

Using Bartering Websites

Bartering websites connect those who have products and services to give with those who need them. Before you sign onto any bartering website, be sure to check it out thoroughly, read all the fine print and contract terms, and use it with caution. As mentioned earlier, these are people you don't know, so it might be unwise to invite a stranger into your home to perform a service. These sites remove themselves from all liability, and much like with any website in which people offer items for sale or themselves for dates, you need to practice smart self-preservation.

Next, don't forget that you can offer your own contract as a term of your barter. Especially with high-value items like professional services, it's a smart move to provide a contract that removes all liability from you. For instance, if the skill you're bartering is your expertise with investments, you have to require a signed contract removing you from any liability resulting from the person's investments. You're just giving a lesson in bonds, for instance, not telling them which bonds to invest in. With a written contract spelling out those terms, you'll stay out of court or defend yourself better if someone does cause you trouble.

TAXES DO APPLY

Remember that the IRS has its eye on bartering, with full tax codes applying to the market value of any trades. When you barter, you will need to report the value of the goods and services you received as part of your gross income. So you must know the value of what you're getting and claim it on your tax return.

Some bartering websites offer trade credits, which you get by offering your services to one member but not taking what they're offering in trade. You hold onto the credits or points you earned, and you can use those credits or points later when you find someone offering something you need for your wedding or your home.

Some sites will offer a tax break if you donate your leftover trade credits to a charity, so look into the fine print of the site to see if that's a viable option for you.

That's Going to Cost You

KEEP TAXES IN MIND FOR BARTERED ITEMS

The IRS will crack down on you if you don't report full market value of the items or services you receive, and you don't want to be subjected to a full IRS audit. So keep careful records down to the dollars and cents, and provide that information to your tax advisor.

SOME BARTERING SITES TO CHECK OUT

Ask friends and family if they use any bartering websites, which ones they love, and which ones they hated. Just like with all aspects of your wedding, it's the first-person experience that sheds great light on a service. Don't base your decision solely on reviews that you see on the bartering website itself, since that company is only going to post glowing reviews. Check with the Better Business Bureau, Yelp, Scam.com, and all other watchdog sites to find out as much as you can about a bartering service before you agree to a trial membership. Some sites are free, and some call for a membership fee, so again, be sure you're knowledgeable on everything expected of you as a member of these bartering communities.

Here are just a few to investigate thoroughly, as their inclusion here does not imply my endorsement:

- BarterQuest.com charges a $9 verification fee at the time of this writing, and it lists what's most in demand on the site in real time, as well as offers photos of items up for barter. Not all barter sites offer images, so members of this community say they chose it for that reason, as well as for the special interest groups it offers, like tech gurus, small business owners, and book lovers, among others.

- U-Exchange.com doesn't charge a fee but makes its money through advertising. It has been named as one of the largest bartering sites, offering both goods and services.

- SwapStyle.com is a fashion-focused bartering site, allowing members to barter clothing, shoes, accessories and cosmetics with other members.

- SwapTree.com lets you swap books, DVDs, music, and more with your free membership.

- Skills2Barter.com matches you up with members offering professional services and skills in exchange for skills or items.

- Craigslist.org has a bartering section on its vast site, with items and services listed for swaps.

- Badabud.com is a social network for creatives, offering artwork, performances, and other artistic services in addition to items. One tier of the system is free, and the premium service allows you to get into the bartering game. The site gives you a chance to earn credits by submitting tips and ideas to the network, and you can use those in part to "pay" for your barter. The site verifies you through your PayPal account just to be sure you're a legitimate person, and it holds all credits in escrow until it hears that both parties are satisfied with their barter. The site says that you can request a partial refund if you're not happy with what you've received.

- SwapAGift.com lets you swap unused gift cards for cash and a percentage of the remaining balance on the card. This isn't a barter, but it's among the most popular "swapping" sites, which is why I placed it here for your research. PlasticJungle.com also accepts gift cards for possible trade or cash.

Also in the swap category is PaperbackSwap.com, where you can list all of your paperbacks and hardcovers, no matter how old but always in good condition, to trade for those other members' list on this free site. I've found $60 wedding books here, in addition to new bestsellers, fabulous cookbooks to help me make recipes for wedding weekend events, and downtime reading to keep my prewedding stress in check. This is a site I use and enjoy. The only cost is postage per trade, the same expense found at all other sites unless free shipping is part of the barter you arrange.

Other bartering sites I've found:

- ThingHeap.com
- Trashbank.com

CLEAR SOME ROOM IN THE BASEMENT

Another source to check out is Freecycle.com, which again is not a barter-ing site, but works in the same "freebie found online" system in which you offer things you don't want and browse through the listed items that other people are recycling here.

It's a simple "come take these chairs" or "come take this Ping-Pong table" mecca that gets items into the hands of nearby people who can use them. You may be able to snag items for your wedding, or items you can trade for items for your wedding. And you can get your attic and basement cleared of all the things you don't need, especially if you'll be moving into a new place after the wedding, combining all of your His and Hers belong-ings and casting off duplicates or outdated items that will soon be replaced by newer models on your wedding registry.

CHAPTER 22

Making Rock-Solid Agreements

As mentioned in the previous two chapters, you have to create a clear, detailed agreement with the person from whom you're getting any free goods or services. It's just smart business sense, and yes, borrowing from *anyone*—even your grandmother—requires extreme clarity to keep this borrow from becoming a nightmare.

Call it a peace-of-mind step for everyone involved.

In the worst of cases, a never-returned item of value is a ticket to court. That adds up to an enormous price tag in lawyer fees, court fees, damages, and your time, because when someone takes you to court, there are plenty of meetings with attorneys, including depositions and other business.

In other cases, which may turn out to still be the worst of cases, your relationship with someone who trusted you to take good care of her lent item is destroyed in a downward spiral of angry e-mails and hurt feelings, which often spiral further down, wider and wider, into a drama of giant proportions when *other* people get involved, taking sides, gossiping, and hurling insults. That can add up to a greater loss than any total of money or time spent in the legal system. A lost relationship has no price tag.

Both of these nightmares can be avoided by creating a rock-solid agreement about the terms of what you're borrowing.

Won't They Be Offended?

If you're worried that presenting your friend, or your grandmother, with a written contract about the terms of what you're borrowing is going to offend them, or make you look silly, get over that worry quickly. Because there's a simpler way to handle this than having your attorney draw up a fifty-page contract.

You just have to put all the details into an e-mail.

When you send an e-mail drafted as a *thank you for agreeing to lend me your (insert item here)* letter, you get all the terms into the letter, and that serves as your agreement. Here's an example:

> *Dear Lisa:*
>
> *Thank you so much for letting me borrow your Mon Cheri veil and headpiece. It's so gorgeous, and I can't wait to wear it on my wedding day. I'm just clarifying what we discussed on Tuesday: I'll pick up the veil and headpiece at your place during Thanksgiving weekend, and I'm keeping it in the top of my closet in a hatbox, not in the basement where things can get damp. So don't worry about that. It'll be perfectly safe. After the wedding, we don't leave for our honeymoon until that Monday, so I'll bring the veil and headpiece back to you in the hatbox on that prior Sunday. And again, as I promised, if any of the appliqués come loose, or if any of the hems fall, I'll pay to have it professionally fixed. Just let me know if you have a seamstress you'd like me to take it to, or if you'd like to take it to someone and have me pay for it. I know, I know . . . I'm just trying to make sure everything's completely arranged so that neither of us has anything to worry about. Thanks again for this great and wonderful honor.*
>
> *Love,*
>
> *(You)*

All the details are there, and you've stated exactly when and how you'll return the item and what you promise to do if there's any *specific* damage to the veil.

Notice I said "specific." You don't want to say vague statements, like if there is any damage to the veil. If a lawyer were looking over your shoulder as you write that, he or she would stop you and tell you to make it more precise.

Now, do you have to go crazy listing imaginative things that could happen to the veil? *If it catches on fire, if a bird flies into it and rips it to shreds, if a food fight breaks out at the reception.* These are highly unlikely, and if you were to put any such occurrences in your letter, the lender would surely get frightened about the safety of her veil, wonder why you're sending a legal letter filled with indemnity clauses, and probably change her mind about lending you that veil.

The bottom line is this: If the item you're borrowing gets damaged or ruined, you're decent enough to have it fixed or replaced. This agreement

Real Stories

ANOTHER WAY FREE LIBRARIES HELP

"We actually looked at the borrowing agreement wording from our local library's website, to make sure we have terms that would protect both sides if there were to be a problem. After all, libraries are in the lending business. It was a big help to see how they spelled out how long something can be borrowed for, what they do to send a reminder if a certain amount of time goes by, and how they assess value of what the borrower would need to replace."—Elizabeth, recent bride from New Jersey

letter is just in place to avoid an open-ended transaction that can cause confusion, stress, and hurt feelings. Never borrow anything without sending an e-mail explaining how you'll care for it, and when and how you'll return it.

And don't worry about offending anyone. Just acknowledge that you're being overly cautious, but that it's because you'll feel better if the lender knows when the item will be returned.

But What If We're Talking Jewelry?

As mentioned earlier—and repeated because it's so important—the lender of fine jewelry, such as a diamond necklace or a set of diamond earrings,

Disaster!

INSURANCE INFORMATION
COULD LEAD TO A NO

The downside to contacting the insurance company about lending out covered jewelry is that the owner might find out that the terms of her insurance means she *can't* lend out the jewelry. The lender might find that the necessary insurance rider costs a lot more than she thought and, with the worries mounting, the lender may need to say *no* to lending the necklace or the sparklers. But it's an important part of protecting everyone, so this step should not be skipped. It would cost you *so* much more if you borrowed an unprotected necklace, lost it, and had to replace that $50,000 piece.

Better to risk getting a no than risk getting financially wiped out by a way-too-risky borrow.

will surely have these valuable items covered in her home insurance. So to keep them, and you, protected, ask the lender to contact her insurance company to get a rider that covers the jewelry when it's lent out. Many insurance companies will provide a form you'll both use to agree to the borrowing of that insured jewelry. The contract is likely to be a serious, legal document with lots of fine print, but it's there to protect you both.

If you don't have any insurance issues, it's still a wise idea to create a written agreement that's as simple as this:

Date: September 24, 2013

We, the undersigned, willingly enter into an agreement in which _____ agrees to lend _____ one Tiffany necklace with three pendant stones, as pictured on the attached page. Tiffany listed this necklace as item #___ on the purchase order, and it is insured in policy # _____ held by _____. _____ agrees to take possession of this necklace on this date, _____, and keep it stored in a locked safe until the wedding date of _____, at which she will wear this necklace during the entire event, returning it personally to _____ at the end of the reception. If _____ is not present at the end of the reception, for such reason as having to leave early for an emergency or for preference, _____ will return the necklace personally by bringing it to _____'s place of residence the day after the wedding, _____. The necklace will be returned by the date of_____ at the very latest.

Notice I put a phrase there in the event of the lender's early departure from the reception. This would prevent the lender from walking up to you on the dance floor, saying goodbye, and holding out her hand for return of the necklace.

Of course, if the lender needs to leave early, she could ask you to walk with her to the bridal suite or the restroom where you can remove the valuable necklace and give it back to her. The privacy of that just-you exchange is very considerate, so if she does walk up to you on the dance floor asking for her necklace, spare yourself the public de-necklacing by asking *her* to join you in the bridal suite. "I have the necklace's velvet case and pouch there and would like to give it to you in that" is all you need to say.

A written agreement protects you in what-if events, and you'll likely not be the type to put yourself into a litigation-magnet situation. For instance, if your friend lends you diamond earrings for your wedding day, you're not going to demand to wear them for the morning-after brunch or the honeymoon. No, you're not a reality show villain or gold digger, so you will hand over the earrings to your obviously cautious or worried friend as soon as you can, because you know how you would feel if you lent a pair

That's Going to Cost You

PERHAPS AN EASIER AGREEMENT WOULD SUFFICE

Not suggesting a written agreement is just asking for bad luck to strike. If the lender doesn't bring up the subject, you should. You might be happy with a simple agreement: *I agree to borrow these earrings on 8/3/13 and return them on 8/14/13.* And sign it.

of precious diamond earrings to a friend, and you don't want to leave them behind when you depart the wedding.

And Sign Here . . .

It's vitally important to provide a space in your written agreement for both you and the lender to sign when the borrowed item is returned. This way, if there's ever any future question about where the necklace is, if months and months down the road, the lender can't find it and remembers lending it to you for your wedding (but not getting it back), you have proof that you did, indeed, return that $10,000 necklace. So set up the bottom of your agreement like this:

Date of Borrow:

_____

Lender

_____

Borrower

Date of Return:

_____

Lender

_____

Borrower

Signatures save your skin, proof in black and white that you held up your end of the bargain. Nothing is left to memory or chance. So remember to put these start and end dates in your borrowing agreement. No matter how valuable the item you're borrowing.

Real Stories

A LENT-NECKLACE HORROR STORY

"I heard about a bride who borrowed a necklace from her friend and returned it, at which point the friend said *this wasn't the necklace she originally lent her.* Turns out, that lender-friend was trying to pull a scam for the price of a more expensive necklace that the bride didn't even borrow. They went to court, where the judge saw photos from the wedding day, showing the original necklace the bride had on—not the more expensive one the lender claimed it to be—and ruled for the bride. It was a nightmare, even though the bride didn't wind up having to pay for the necklace. She still had to get a lawyer and spend a lot of time fighting this bogus situation. So take this advice: Always attach a close-up, detailed photo of what you're borrowing with any lender agreement."—Stephanie, recent bride from New York City

When You're Mailing Something Back

If the lender lives far away, conduct a mail transaction using, without fail, an insured and trackable system. If the lender is doing the mailing, request the tracking number. When you receive the item, send an e-mail right away with your thanks for sending it, and your compliments on how gorgeous it is.

When you're shipping the item back, use the insured and trackable system, and send the lender the tracking number via e-mail. Again, that e-mail is proof and a paper trail that you have kept your end of the bargain.

When the Deal Is Done

After your dream wedding day, all items are to be returned as soon as humanly possible. There's no excuse for any delays. Claiming to have so much to do is not an excuse when someone's waiting for her item back, and no one should have to call you to ask where the item is. Make it a high, high priority to return all borrows before you even start setting up your home with all of those wedding gifts.

And no matter what the value of the item lent—from a tablecloth to a ruby tennis bracelet—send a thank-you note separate from your official wedding thank-you note, along with a thank-you gift. The lender will be so appreciative of your great manners and generosity.

Some of the most popular thank-you gifts for borrowed items include:

- A box of chocolates or truffles

- A bottle of wine or champagne

- A framed photo of the item as part of your wedding day—if it's something you're wearing, send a photo of you *and the lender,* not just you with the earrings on

Real Stories

CHOOSE A MEANINGFUL, PERSONALIZED CHARITABLE DONATION

"My aunt is very eco-conscious, so I sent her a note saying that I made a donation to the Arbor Day Foundation, and had ten trees planted—in her name—in a forest in California, to help replant after wildfires. She *loved* it."—Chloe, recent bride from Savannah

- A framed photo of the lender and his or her spouse or partner

- A charitable contribution made in the lender's name

If you have further concerns about striking a legal agreement for a borrowed item, talk to an attorney to find out about any specific language that you should include in your contract or documents. Different states have different laws about lending items and lending money, and you'll want to be sure you have the details of your agreement spelled out in the safest and most specific way possible.

Part Five: Win It!

Brides walk away from bridal shows with some spectacular prizes. Imagine *winning* a five-star honeymoon at an exclusive celebrity-favorite island resort, or a $10,000 wedding gown, or complete hair and makeup for you and your bridesmaids on the wedding morning. In this section, you'll get the inside scoop on how to improve your odds of winning lots of prizes and freebies for your wedding.

Speaking of prizes, don't forget to use that bridal luck of yours to enter sweepstakes at bridal magazine websites, as well as at other contest sources you'll find here. They're places you might never have thought to look, but you could win $100,000 because you did. Those prizes—$10,000, $25,000, $100,000—add up to a completely free wedding and honeymoon, plus amazing things for your home and life together.

Bring on the *Win It!* freebie ideas.

CHAPTER 23

Freebies from Bridal Shows

A five-star all-inclusive honeymoon, a free designer gown, a free veil, free *shoes,* free party bus use for your bachelorette party, free hair and makeup styling, free dance classes—these are just some of the prizes that brides and grooms win at bridal shows and expos.

Here's your first priceless tip of this section, something to give you an edge on the competition: You can get *amazing* things for free, just by attending your local bridal shows and expos—*and staying until the end.*

I can't tell you how many bridal shows I've been to where the organizers conducted the door prize drawings for a dozen or more fantastic prizes and the winning brides weren't there. After the third shout-out for a prize winner, the organizer went to the next name in the hat. And the next, and the next, until the very patient and very smart winner jumped up and squealed at taking home her second prize of the night. Now she had a free honeymoon *and* a free party bus for her bachelorette party, and there were still prizes to give away.

Surprised at how big these prizes are? We've come a long way since the days of the door prize being scented candles. In today's hotly competitive wedding world, vendors are bringing the goods and putting *valuable* products and services up for the winning. One wedding vendor dished: "Giving out a great prize is the smartest way I know to get my business tons of publicity. When the winning bride tweets or Facebooks to all of her local friends that she won my videography package, I get tons of hits on my website from all of those friends checking me out. It's better than any ad I could pay for, and I can sometimes book five or six paying gigs just from giving away one free package to a bride at a bridal show."

That's not the only reason many wedding vendors are offering better door prizes than ever. Some bridal shows *require* vendors to provide a door prize over $100 in value, or more in some instances. The show organizers know that they're competing with other bridal shows' reputations, and that brides have been to shows that featured underwhelming prizes like little baggies of candy or that scented candle and they've also been to shows that offered an hour of consulting from a celebrity wedding expert. Show organizers want to be in, or closer to, the latter category, so they've made an industry-wide push for better door prizes, which means you get better things for free.

Some bridal show organizers are even offering cut rates for vendors to display at the show, in exchange for a door prize valued at more than $200. They want the brides and grooms to be wowed by the phenomenal door prizes and rave to their friends about the show. Sure enough, more and more local wedding couples attend the following weekend's show. It's a smart strategy for the show organizer, the vendors, and you when you win those seven days in Antigua.

But, you most often have to be there at the end of the show to pick up your prize. Don't be the bride who isn't there to claim the freebie. And if you're there at the end, you may be that fifth name called who gets to take home the prize that someone else left behind.

The key to snagging freebies at bridal shows is to go to several of them. TheWeddingReport.com recently ran a survey on the topic of bridal shows and found that 80 percent of brides and grooms said they did or would attend a bridal show, and on average, they went to 2.8 bridal shows, spending an average of $15.50 on bridal show tickets.

What to Expect

THE TYPES OF VENDORS AT BRIDAL SHOWS

- Accessories
- Bakeries
- Banking
- Beauty & Skin Care
- Bridal Gowns/Wedding Dresses
- Bridesmaid Dresses
- Catering
- Ceremony Locations
- Cosmetic Surgery and Dentistry
- Cruises
- Dance Lessons
- DJs
- Entertainment
- Favors
- Financial Services
- Florists
- Guest Accommodations
- Health Club and Spa
- Honeymoons
- Hotel/Reception Sites
- House and Home
- Insurance
- Invitations
- Jewelry and Wedding Rings
- Music
- Officiants
- Party Rentals
- Photography
- Real Estate
- Reception Locations
- Rehearsal Dinner
- Resorts
- Transportation
- Travel
- Tuxedoes
- Videography
- Wedding Cakes
- Wedding Coordinators
- Wedding Gift Registry

Real Stories

BRING MORE PEOPLE, WIN MORE PRIZES

"I paid for my bridesmaids' tickets, so they could attend the show with me. Some of them won great prizes and chose to give them to me. The one who won the mani/pedi at the spa kept hers, which was fine with me. My girls are spending a lot to be in my wedding."—Nancy, recent bride from Virginia

To improve your odds of winning freebies, try to attend at least three bridal shows, more if you have the time. Your groom doesn't want to endure *another* few hours of Bridal Central? Take your maid of honor, your mom, his mom, or just stop in by yourself. When you go with your ladies, you all enjoy a fun day out, indulge in some free champagne and hors d'oeuvres, hear some fun music from the band, and take in the energy of a great bridal show. Plus, your girls can take home product-stuffed goodie bags—and some shows really know how to attract designer name cosmetics and nail polishes, top-brand stockings, and other beauty and spa essentials. And, of course, having five ladies with you means your group gets five extra chances to win door prizes. If your maid of honor wins a free veil, she may very well give that gift card to you. If your maid of honor is planning her own wedding right now, this bridal expo day turns out to be a pretty sweet freebie source for her as well.

What's Up for Grabs?

Most bridal shows feature door prizes offered by each of their vendors, plus one or more big prizes provided by the show itself. The free honeymoon is usually the domain of the show organizers, who have relationships with resort brands donating a free trip for every show. You may get a week at a fabulous island resort, a cruise, or a four-day trip that would make a great pre-honeymoon, girls' weekend, or mini-moon.

Here, by select vendor category, are some of the most-often-seen door prizes offered:

- *Wedding Coordinators:* Free wedding book or organizer, free seating chart software, free day-of coordination when you book with them, free one-hour consultation to help book your vendors when you book with them, free bridal shower consultation when you book your wedding with them (this is a great, smart way to help your bridesmaids find budget resources and great vendors), free planning help for your mom to put together the rehearsal dinner when you book with them.

- *Florists:* Free engagement party corsage, free small floral centerpiece (ideal for the rehearsal dinner), free dozen roses, free men's boutonnieres when you book with them, free flower girl basket when you book with them.

What to Expect

THE TWO TYPES OF FREEBIES

Seeing a trend here? Many vendors will offer the straight-up freebie, such as those dozen roses, and many will offer the freebie that you can get when you book them to work your wedding. These wins mean you get some pretty valuable items as freebies in your wedding package. The average cost of boutonnieres, according to TheWeddingReport .com? More than $75. That's a nice win.

- *Photographers:* Free photo album (great for a grandparents' book of wedding photos), free photo frame, free engagement photo session when you book with them, free bride's portrait when you book with them, free parents' album when you book with them, twenty-five free 5 x 7 inch prints when you book with them (prints are pricy—this is a fabulous freebie), free upgrade to a leather-bound photo album when you book with them (again, this is a high-value win—albums can cost $700, if not twice that!), free monogramming on your photo album when you book with them, free set of your print proofs when you book with them (this one is a treasure, since you can frame print proofs for friends, or make photo albums for your bridal party, your parents, and yourselves, saving you thousands of dollars).

- *Videographers:* Free bridal-themed jewel case for your wedding DVD, free video montage of your baby photos for use on your personal website or at your wedding celebrations, free special effects editing when you book with them, one extra hour free when you book with them (that can be $500 or more in some cases).

- *Cake Bakers:* Free round cake for your engagement party or bridal shower, free dozen cupcakes, free cake topper (these freebie cake toppers are fun for your engagement party, rehearsal dinner, or bridal shower—you'll likely want to pick out your own style of topper for your wedding cake), free upgrade to premium cake flavors and fillings when you book with them, free chocolate-covered strawberries with your cake order.

- *Transportation Companies:* One extra hour free when you book with them, free champagne and snacks in the limousine when you book with them, free red carpet and champagne stand when you book with them, free upgrade to a stretch limousine when you book with them.

Real Stories

ONE WIN, TEN USES

"We won a cupcake tree at a bridal show, and we used it at *everything*: the engagement party, the bridal shower, the wedding morning breakfast, the after-party, the morning-after breakfast. Considering I've seen those for $30 at stores, we just got $150 use out of it . . . so far! It may not be a huge prize, but it definitely was a great prize for me!" —Denise, recent bride from Philadelphia

- *Beauty Salons:* Free mani/pedi, free trial makeup session, free eyebrow shaping, free basket of salon-quality beauty products and styling tools, free trial hairstyle session when you book with them, free champagne at your hairstyle trial appointment when you book with them, free second trial hairstyle session, for your maid of honor or your mom, when you book with them.

- *Entertainers:* Free pianist during your cocktail hour when you book with them, one extra hour free when you book with them, free use of their flat screen for displaying your video at the reception when you book with them.

- *Favor Artists:* Packs of free truffles, brownies, frosted cookies, wedding-themed coasters, cake pops, personalized ribbon or wrapping paper, personalized favor bags, a pair of *Bride* and *Groom* wooden hangers for your wedding day gown and tux photos (this is a favorite prize).

A big trend right now is for wedding vendors to give out something other than a gift card for their own services. They'll add on a great extra

---

What to Expect

STOP BY VENDOR TABLES
YOU MIGHT NOT THINK YOU NEED

Vendors you're not very interested in might have some great prizes at their tables. If you're passing the fifth wedding photographer's well-lit table of albums and flat-screen slide show behind him, slow down and see what his door prize is. It could be something really good.

---

prize in addition to their gift card. *"I know that many brides and grooms come to bridal shows for specific things, like ideas for their flowers or to see the entertainers, after they've already started booking plans for their weddings. They've already booked their photographer, so that percentage of the brides and grooms won't be lining up to meet me,"* says a wedding photographer in Philadelphia. *"But if I have a big sign saying my door prize is a $100 gift card to Williams-Sonoma, they sign up to win it. I'm then on their radar in case they do want to check out photographers, and—since I know that most brides have about six other engaged friends—they may tell their friends about me, Facebook that they won a great prize from me, and wish they hadn't already signed with another photographer. I get lots of interest calls from that situation. And I wouldn't have it if I didn't do the retail store gift card."* So now you know the strategy many wedding experts use at bridal shows so that you can potentially score your unity candle for free from Williams-Sonoma.

Freebies and Prizes at Upscale Bridal Shows

You'll see some bridal shows pop up with free entry, some that charge a small entry fee, and some that charge a heftier amount because they're so-called upscale shows. These elite shows often attract celebrity wedding experts like Colin Cowie, Preston Bailey, and Sylvia Weinstock, and they offer spectacular catering and champagne (unlike the free bridal shows that offer slices of cake and that's about it).

These shows have some phenomenal prizes, offered by the vendors and by the organizers. At the Wedding Salon (weddingsalon.com), an upscale bridal show in New York, Los Angeles, and other big cities, for instance, recent prizes have been dream honeymoons to exotic locales, designer wedding gowns, designer shoes, designer invitations, and more. Each prize saves the winner thousands of dollars.

What to Expect

At the Wedding Salon's most recent splashy event, the upscale prize packages included:

- *Four* brides and grooms winning luxury weekend getaways at four-diamond inns.

- A four-day, three-night, gourmet, all-inclusive getaway at the four-diamond El Dorado Spa & Resort by Karisma.

- A $300 groom's cake made by the *Food Network's Cake Challenge* star Leo Sciancalepore of *A Little Cake*.

- Designer framed table cards in a beach theme, created by OliverInk.

- A night on the town in a chauffeured stretch limousine for six hours.

And more . . . visit WeddingSalon.com to see what's new in its Gifting Suite.

Yes, there is an entrance fee to this class of elite bridal show, but—here's the good news—when you friend these shows on Facebook and follow them on Twitter, you can often win free tickets (or get a discount). Another inside secret: Wedding coordinators and other vendors often score tickets to give away. So put this book down and contact the vendors you've booked, asking if they have any tickets to the big bridal shows. They, too, announce their stack of free or discounted tickets on their Facebook pages, so friend them as well.

Obviously, you don't want to go overboard in trying to get into the show for free. Inside those doors organizers try to make a little money for their time, and vendors paid a lot for their display booths. If you happen to chance upon a free entry, that's terrific. If not, remember that the price of your ticket gets you into a wonderland of potential prize wins, some fine bubbly and delectable cake, and a swag bag filled with fantastic freebies.

Real Stories

SOMETIMES VENDORS CAN GET YOU FREE BRIDAL SHOW TICKETS

"I asked my florist if she knew anything about the big bridal show coming up, and she said that a friend of hers—a favors artist—was going to be showing there. She made a phone call and scored me two free tickets through her friend. I loved her favors, so my maid of honor took her card to hire her for the bridal shower favors."—Lisa, recent bride from Vermont

About That Swag Bag

Getting the goodie bag is one reason brides go to so many shows. Yes, you'll get a lot of brochures from vendors, some lollipops and baggies of chocolates, a pen with a company name on it—but at many shows, remember, organizers now require items of substance for inclusion in the goodie bags. They've heard brides at past shows grumbling that all they got was a bag full of brochures, so bridal expo chiefs have raised the bar. Now, there's more substance in the bags, so you might get a nail polish from the nail salon, a set of stylish headbands from the hair salon, a garter from the bridal gown shop (saving you more than $40 in some instances if you like this one), a cute little photo flip book from the photographer, a wine bottle stopper from the wine bar, a gourmet bar of chocolate, and the usually included bridal magazine, among other freebies.

How Do You Win?

The methods of winning at any type of bridal show vary. You might be automatically entered to win the grand door prize just by buying your ticket to the show, or if it's a free show, by providing your name and e-mail address to gain entry. That information goes on a valuable data sheet called a Leads List that bridal shows sell to wedding vendors. Since you're already going to get lots of e-mails and postcards from wedding vendors, you might as well enjoy the chance to win that honeymoon or that $350 crystal-studded tiara.

Another way to win is by signing onto contact information sheets at each vendor's table. They get your name, address, and e-mail, and you might win their prize.

Another way to win is by playing the game. When entertainers take the stage to perform their fifteen-minute act in front of the bridal show crowd, they often ask for a volunteer to come up and sing with them, dance with them, or be serenaded. When you're game, and a good

What to Expect

SAVE YOUR HAND WITH THIS
CONTEST-ENTRY STRATEGY

When you go to a bridal show, particularly a big bridal show such as those that sell out a huge convention hall, you'll write your name, address, and e-mail a lot to enter for those freebies. That's why I suggest bringing lots of your return address labels, such as those that come in the mail with solicitations for donations to various charities. You might not plan to use the return address labels with the polar bears on them, but they'll serve you well—and save your hand—when you affix *those* onto each entry sheet, and just pen in your e-mail address. Some brides and grooms even print up label sheets, including their e-mail, on their home computer. A quick tip: If you're going to set up a special e-mail account just for your bridal tasks, like entering contests (and keeping all of those wedding vendor e-mail solicitations out of your personal or work inboxes), be sure you check that side e-mail account at least every three days so you don't miss out on a freebie.

participant, the entertainers appreciate your saving their hides and helping them put on a good show. So they will often hand you a gift certificate for an add-on to their package, or something from a partner of theirs, such as a free dinner at a local restaurant. The plan is that the crowd will be so enthralled by the show they—and you—put on that they'll book the act *and* be impressed by your prize. Should you book them, too? We'll get into that later in this chapter.

And then there's the spin-the-wheel win. You step up to the vendor's table, where you'll get your turn giving the carnival game wheel a spin. It's a popular strategy used by many vendors: If you feel you've *won* something by *doing* something (in this case, spinning the wheel), then you have power. You feel connected to the prize you've won, because you earned it. Considering the prize might be a free groom's tuxedo when you rent at least four others from that tux shop, the plan is for you to say, "Hey, I've got this freebie, so we should probably book with this tux shop!" But hold on a second, because here's your warning.

If you don't plan to use the freebie you've been handed, for whatever reason—perhaps you've booked your band or photographer, or you simply didn't like the particular style of the DJ—get yourself some great karma by handing that gift card off to another engaged friend or relative who might be able to use it. Keep in mind that the company might have your name

Disaster!

JUST A REMINDER: CHECK OUT CONTEST-WIN COMPANIES THOROUGHLY

Not all freebies are good freebies. Whenever you're planning anything for your wedding, you always have to invest a lot of time and energy into checking out the company, making sure it has a good reputation, finding out how well it provides its services, if it is a member of an association, if it has been in business for a long time. So accept that gift card or certificate with a smile, and consider it a *Happy Maybe*. *Maybe* the company is great. You'll find out when you compare it to other companies and do your full research.

attached to that freebie, with rules that it's nontransferable. But it can't hurt to check out the possibility of your friend getting the freebie. Call the company to see if it will allow it.

Finding These Bridal Shows

You might know the most well-known names in bridal shows, such as the Great Bridal Expo and the Wedding Salon, but on any given weekend, there are thousands of bridal shows taking place at hotels and conference centers all over the country. Here's how to find them:

- Go to the website for your regional bridal magazine. It might be *Portland Bride and Groom, New Jersey Bride,* or even a wider region like *Southern Bride.* There, you'll find a long list of the bridal shows taking place in your area, with dates up to three or four months in advance and links to the bridal show's website for buying tickets. Many regional bridal magazines offer a special "reader discount code" that might get you a nice percentage off your ticket fee or grant you two tickets for the price of one. Good Karma Alert: As the

That's Going to Cost You

DON'T TRY TO SELL YOUR FREEBIE

You can get in a lot of trouble if you go online to sell your freebie coupon. There are all kinds of laws prohibiting that, and the fine print on the back of the card probably has a long list of Don'ts, including just this very thing. So if no one can use it, and the company won't honor it for anyone but you, it's not something that can do anyone much good.

bride bringing your maid of honor or mom, it's quite nice to give *her* the freebie ticket and pay for your own.

- Also, go to the big bridal magazine websites, like *Brides, Bridal Guide,* and *The Knot,* where you'll also find bridal show listings shown by region, and, heck, look the shows up on Facebook and Twitter. When you click "like" or follow them, you may be granted free or discounted tickets to their show, as a thank-you for being a fan.

- Hotels and restaurants also host bridal expos, large and small. So check out their websites, Facebook pages, and Twitter accounts to learn about bridal shows they have planned, and again, possibly get free or cut-rate tickets. Check with your local tourism office at TOWD.com. The offices always have lists of what's going on all over town, and their site or staff can point you to upcoming showcases. Some tourism offices even have those prized free or discount tickets.

- Google "online bridal show," which is trending as a unique bridal expo format. *Martha Stewart Weddings* recently put together an online bridal show, which is a special website offering virtual "visits" with vendors and recorded seminars by top wedding experts. And yes, you can win excellent prizes for "attending." Even if you were in your pajamas in front of your computer. True, you get no free cake or champagne, but it's a different spin on the traditional bridal show that might just introduce you to the perfect vendors for your wedding's style.

- Coupon sites are also great sources for bridal show information and freebie tickets. For instance, go to RetailMeNot.com, which often has coupon codes for two free tickets to various bridal shows. I visited at the time of this writing and saw two free tickets to the Great Bridal Expo—and while I was there, I discovered several sweepstakes I could enter to win even more free wedding and honeymoon prizes.

Real Stories

GO TO A SPECIALIZED SHOW

"We found it easier to focus on the destination wedding and honeymoon travel topic when the entire show was just about that. At regular bridal expos, there was so much going on, the loud music, the fashion shows, servers coming by with food and cake—it was sensory overload. And there were only three big resorts displaying there. At the honeymoon expo, there were hundreds, so we were really able to look at their videos and photos, collect up bunches of their packets, compare them, and stay on the one topic fully. We found our dream honeymoon spot, too, and won a really nice designer travel bag as a door prize."
—Sara, recent bride from Seattle

- Ask your wedding coordinator and wedding vendors for the schedules of any bridal shows they would recommend. This is a smart step, since these pros know which shows are good and which can be skipped. They've been to all the shows, either displaying or checking out the scene, and they will be happy to steer you away from disappointing, waste-of-time bridal shows that offer no freebies and attract some not-so-professionals since their vendor tables are priced so cheaply.

- Check out the top bridal blogs, such as OneWed.com, BridalTweet .com, and StyleMePretty.com to see their listings of by-state bridal shows, and even wedding registry sites offer bridal show listings. At BedBathandBeyond.com, for example, you'll find a current, updated pdf of bridal shows and expos taking place all over the country. (The Resources section of this book includes a listing of the top wedding registry websites.)

- Attend honeymoon expos and showcases, or travel showcases, at your local convention center. You might see these on the bridal websites, but more often, you'll discover them on the websites for the convention centers themselves. Travel companies, resorts, cruise lines, and others display at these big shows, and the door prizes can be quite amazing. The same goes for branded "destination wedding showcases" run by or in conjunction with destination wedding magazines.

Other sources listing shows: the events calendar on your local regional magazine's website, where smaller events just miss the print magazine's listing deadline; your local Junior League (AJLI.org), which might host an event for charity; and bridal gown salon, floral designer, and other vendor sites and Facebook pages that invite you to see them at the show.

Look in the Resources section of this book to find national bridal show websites that sponsor them, list them, and perhaps even offer free tickets to them.

What to Expect

ANY WINNINGS HAVE TAX IMPLICATIONS

Any prize won has to be reported as gross income, so if you win a honeymoon valued at $10,000 or a dress in that price range, you must report it in your tax return. You could be responsible for up to a third or more of that value in state and federal taxes, depending on your tax rate.

CHAPTER 24

Entering Contests and Giveaways

Expand your contest horizons and you could win *really* big prizes like $250,000, a new house, a luxury vehicle, or an entirely free destination wedding on a private island where celebrities often marry. This chapter rounds up some of the top contest, sweepstake, and giveaway sources to help you use that bridal luck for big, big winnings. A check for $100,000 at prize time? That grand prize can make your entire wedding *and* honeymoon free.

Of course, the prizes you'll find on each of these sites vary. Some are for jaw-dropping amounts of cash, and some are fun little freebies like a bottle of nail polish. Some will hook up your bridesmaids with free dresses, and some will supply you with maxi pads for the rest of your life. Whatever the prize, the winnings count as freebies for your wedding if they free up money you would have otherwise spent on non-wedding purchases. A $500 prize to your grocery store? That's five weekly food shops free, and $500 into your wedding budget. A $50 box of truffles? That's either a mental health treat for you, or a thank-you gift for your mom or wedding coordinator.

No matter what you win, you *win*.

Just keep in mind that, again, the prizes you win *must* be reported as taxable income, part of your gross earnings, to keep you in the clear with the IRS.

Make the Most of Contest Opportunities

Don't limit yourself to the bridal magazines' websites for entering sweepstakes. As you'll see here, there are tons of media sources that make it easy for you to enter their contests, and some of them are in categories you might not have even thought of. A cooking magazine's grand prize of two weeks in Italy can become your honeymoon. A parenting magazine's grand prize of $10,000 to remodel a nursery can be used to finance a destination wedding. A home improvement website's spring cleaning giveaway might just land you $20,000 and all new top-of-the-line tools.

I searched the many sweepstakes sites out there to deliver the most reputable contest sources and decided to stick with magazines, lifestyle networks, and a few proven legitimate media groups that run solid contests and deliver on their prizes. Remember, the world is full of scammers, and you don't want to get taken by a fake contest that collects your personal information and never sends anyone a prize. Stick with well-known brand names and media empires, and you will be safest.

What to Expect

KNOW THE DIFFERENT WAYS TO ENTER AND WIN

Each magazine, whether it's bridal, women's, parenting, travel, or others, is most likely to run its giveaways in at least five ways: in the print magazine, on the magazine's website (sweepstakes page), in the magazine's blog, on the magazine's Facebook page, and on the magazine's Twitter account. So bookmark and subscribe to all, to make sure you have access to the entry page, especially if it's a one-entry-a-day contest.

Now, before we get into where these contests and giveaways are listed, let's first make sure you're loaded with smart strategies for entering the contests:

- First, create a special e-mail account that you'll use to register for contests, and where related sales-mail will arrive, rather than jamming up your personal e-mail account. And never enter from your work e-mail account, since your bosses may monitor it.

- Enter every day, if it's a one-a-day entry process. Bookmark the entry page, and fill in the necessary information. Some sites, like BHG .com, operate off of your membership information so all you have to do is click on the contest and then click submit. It knows where you are and how to reach you. Other sites, like HGTV.com, require you to fill in your name, address, and e-mail, and then the next time you come back to enter, all you have to fill in is your e-mail address. It, too, knows who you are.

- Enter from start to finish. Day One to the last day of any sweepstakes gets an entry from you. There's no science that says your odds are better by entering at the end of the month.

- Make it a daily ritual. My first-thing-in-the-morning ritual is sitting down at my computer, going to HGTV.com and BHG.com, and clicking to enter all of the daily-entry sweepstakes I'd love to win. It's a relatively low-thought process that gets me warmed up, and I thrive on the optimism of entering sweepstakes. Each entry gets me envisioning that knock on the door and a five-foot check with my name on it, and that's not a bad way to start my day. I suggest it for you, or maybe you'd like your dose of optimism to come in the evening, or during your 4 p.m. sugar crash.

- Get creative and write well. Some contests require you to share an anecdote or write about how you would use the prize money.

Real Stories

DON'T JUST GO FOR BRIDAL ITEMS

"One of my favorite contests out there right now is the *Food Network* magazine column that asks you to name a multi-ingredient dish or sandwich. You get a couple of hundred dollars in Food Network products as your prize, but it's so fun to dream up catchy titles for that concoction their chefs have put together!"—Alan, recent groom from Atlanta

Creativity does count, and some media sources bring in published authors and other experts to judge the entries. So get clever, title your anecdote well, and make sure your write-up is free of grammar or spelling mistakes, amuses as it informs, and stands out from a sea of other entries. Watch the movie *The Prize Winner of Defiance, Ohio,* starring Julianne Moore as a talented writer/punster who wins prize after prize, to get a feel for what I'm talking about. Short and sweet catchy sayings or non-cliché mini-essays will always boost your odds of winning.

• Play by the rules. If the contest says one entry per household, you had better believe they have a team of experts making sure that the winner—perhaps you—didn't enter from six different e-mail addresses in the same home. They employ companies to verify the winners, and those companies will check those things out, so practice good ethics and your resulting good karma can make you the winner of cash, cars, and more.

• Pick the style of contest you like best. Is it click-and-enter? Or "send in your best recipe to win $500"? Is it easy for you to record and

That's Going to Cost You

PRACTICE GOOD CONTEST ETIQUETTE

Think hard about those contests that have you posting your project photos or videotaped tips and then ask you to have all of your friends and family "vote" for your entry every day. That's quite an imposition on their time and can make you a daily annoyance when you're constantly pleading with people to vote for you over the course of weeks, if not longer. So think about the high price of this type of contest before you ask your networks to vote for you.

upload your video entry, in which you explain—and act out a cute skit on—why you should be chosen as the bride who wins a $15,000 wedding dress? What's your creation-factor for these entries? Knowing what you're good at and what you enjoy can streamline your contest-entering plans and perhaps even improve your odds of winning.

- Look at the little guys, too. While the big bridal magazines run huge contests, smaller wedding blogs that are in the process of growing and attracting corporate partners give away some excellent prizes—and the entry pool is much smaller than that of the mega-media sites.

- Tell your inner circle to send you links to any great contests or sweepstakes they see. Perhaps they subscribe to a fashion magazine or blog and just know you'd love the chance to win a pair of Louboutins for your wedding day. If you send out an e-mail letting your loved ones know that you're having fun entering contests, they can forget about that "nah, she probably wouldn't want this" hesitation and send it your way. And always offer to return the favor when you see any contests they would like.

- Subscribe to magazines' contests and sweepstakes newsletters. Most of them offer a specialty e-newsletter sent weekly *to an e-mail account you check out weekly.* The freshest news comes to you right away, and you get to enter during the full course of the contests' running.

Where the Sweepstakes Are

These are just a few of the sensational sources I've found for scoping out sweepstakes, starting with "the usual suspects" of bridal magazines and websites, and expanding outward to magazines and sites you might not automatically think about. For instance, if you're not a parent, you can still enter sweepstakes hosted by *Parents* magazine. Travel, food, and other magazines often run multiple, overlapping contests, always offering some phenomenal prizes.

For each bridal magazine, remember to look in the print pages and on the official website, site blogs, Facebook page, and Twitter feeds for the latest and upcoming giveaways. Some bridal magazines reward their social media followers with exclusive-to-them giveaways, so you don't want to miss those.

BRIDAL MAGAZINES

Sites like Brides.com, BridalGuide.com, TheKnot.com, GetMarried.com, and more often run single-item giveaways such as a honeymoon, as well as combination giveaways. For instance, you'll find sweepstakes for flight-included seven-day honeymoons at luxury resorts, plus all meals and spa treatments, all-inclusive destination weddings at exotic locales plus adventure outings like swimming with dolphins, $10,000 wedding gowns and beauty treatments at an elite beauty salon, a $150,000 wedding plus several hundred dollars to spend at a department store, your entire invitations package plus custom logo design, designer wedding shoes and a custom bra-fitting, plus shapewear, and more.

While the major national bridal magazines attract big-name resort giveaways and designer prizes, regional bridal magazines also offer designer gowns, shoes, and equally impressive honeymoons and destination wedding packages. Find your regional bridal magazine through a Google search, and check out its offerings.

BRIDAL BLOGS

They may not be in print, but bridal blogs, as you know, have large numbers of followers, they're ever present in social media, and they attract big-time

What to Expect

WIN FABULOUS PRIZES AT TWITTER PARTIES

Most bridal magazines have learned that Twitter parties are a wildly popular way to garner buzz, get fans interacting with their editors and guest wedding professionals, get questions answered in real time, and give away some amazing prizes. So keep an eye on your favorite wedding magazines' and blogs' sites to see when they have a Twitter party scheduled. Jump online, and follow the directions. You're often asked to re-tweet (RT) snippets from the chat to be entered in the giveaway. Winners are often selected from participants and RTers at random via a prize-selection app, or the organizers select winners from participants who posted comments or asked questions most often.

companies for some big-time giveaways. For instance, BrokeAssBride.com attracts fun and offbeat prizes, such as organic white pearl earrings and funky dresses. Wishpot.com recently ran a wedding luxuries giveaway featuring shopping sprees for a gown, a harpist for your ceremony, and cuff links for the groom and groomsmen. WeddingBee.com offered a jaw-dropping Disney Weddings package that would make all kinds of wedding wishes come true. It also runs contests for everything from wedding gowns to iTunes gift cards.

One of my favorite sweepstakes sources is BridalTweet.com, where hundreds of wedding bloggers, magazines, vendors, and Etsy artists list their current sweepstakes and contests. Just click on "Wedding Ideas For Brides," go to the "Contests and Sweepstakes" page, and you'll find a long, long list of contests you might wish to enter. You'll find gift cards for invitations and favors, jewelry, and more, often announced by bloggers who hit a milestone number of followers and celebrate by giving a little something away. Not all of the prizes are "a little something." Here, too, you'll find groups of vendor-friends joining together to load up the prize package with hundreds of dollars worth of prizes.

WOMEN'S MAGAZINES

If it's cash you'd like to win, the place to go is to the women's magazine websites. You simply fill out a free membership to the magazine's site—your name, address, and e-mail—and you're in. Being a member speeds up your entry process, since the sites remember you and all you have to do is click on each sweepstakes entry button, then confirm your entry. There's no tedious filling in of your personal information in most contests.

Even better, many of these magazines are published as part of the same parent company. So if you go to the *Better Homes and Gardens* website (bhg.com), you'll see and enter contests for *Family Circle, Parents,* and *Traditional Home.* Here's my list of favorite women's magazines with spectacular giveaways:

- *Better Homes and Gardens*

- *Family Circle*

- *Ladies' Home Journal*

- *Redbook*

- *Woman's Day*

- *First*

- *All You*

As for their prizes, I've seen everything from $25,000 to $100,000 cash prizes, new kitchen remodels, new wardrobes, new cars, and vacations that can be used for a honeymoon, destination wedding, girls' getaway, mini-moon, or pre-honeymoon. The trips are quite amazing, located all over the country and on tropical islands.

While many of these contests are click-to-enter, some are of the recipe variety. For instance, *Better Homes and Gardens* runs a monthly, themed recipe contest that you can enter online. I actually won $500 in this one, with my Steak Carbonnade recipe, so I can attest that people really do win.

Speaking of recipes, while they're not necessarily women's magazines exclusively, check out the many foodie-centric magazines like *Bon Appétit, Cooking Light, Food & Wine, Wine Spectator, Saveur,* and others. They, too, offer prizes beyond the usual skillets and panini makers. Cash also makes the rounds there, as do food-centric vacations.

TRAVEL MAGAZINES

Travel magazines get some amazing vacation packages to give away. Frommer's *Budget Travel,* for instance, recently ran a big sweepstakes for a "Dream Trip to South Africa," including round-trip coach-class airfare for two from New York City or Washington, D.C., to Cape Town, South

Africa; two nights' hotel stay in Cape Town; two nights' stay in South African wine country; two nights' stay at the Sanbona Wildlife Preserve; two game drives per day at the Sanbona Wildlife Preserve; breakfast at Cape Town and Wine Country hotels; and all meals at the Sanbona Wildlife Preserve. The value of this pretty package was $5,000. Other travel magazines to check out include *Condé Nast Traveler* and *Travel & Leisure*.

Also in the travel category are the top destination wedding magazines, such as *Destination I Do* magazine and *Destination Weddings and Honeymoons,* both garnering top travel packages from some of the world's most luxurious locales and top-tier resorts, offering both free weddings and honeymoons, with additional perks for your guests. Add these to your bookmark collection, and enter as often as you're allowed. Even if your honeymoon is booked, these trips would make a fabulous second honeymoon when taken before a year passes.

LIFESTYLE MEDIA

I mentioned *Traditional Home* magazine as part of the circle of women's magazine contests, and it's one of the many lifestyle magazines, sites, blogs, Facebook pages, and Twitter feeds that can deliver anything from cash to a newly designed living room, a remodel of your kitchen, and other fabulous prizes that let you use your wedding gift money for something other than a pricy home re-do project. Also in this class are the magazines *Southern Living, Midwest Living, Cottages and Bungalows, Romantic Homes, Dwell,* and more.

LIFESTYLE NETWORKS

If you were to win the HGTV Dream Home, not only would you get a styled-out mansion filled with fabulous furniture and kitchen appliances, the grand prize also usually comes with a $500,000 cash prize and a car or truck. Not a bad haul for using the site's easy-entry method every day. You just fill out your information once, and then each time you return to the page, you enter your e-mail address and it fills in the rest. HGTV also gives away the Blog Cabin, an Urban Escape apartment in a major city, and lots of other prizes during the year. DIY Network is another site to check, since it, too, runs cash and prizes sweepstakes through the year, also with the auto-entry tool that makes it fast and easy to get your chance in for the day.

Food Network runs star-promoted sweepstakes for such things as cash, new kitchen appliances, trips to Tuscany, tickets to the *Food and Wine Classic* in Aspen, signed copies of celebrity chefs' cookbooks, and more. When Food Network runs its *Next Food Network Star* series, you can often enter to win prizes related to that hit show. The cash and trips help make your wedding and honeymoon freebies, and the home-oriented prizes give you freebies for life after the wedding. Your cash wedding gifts can then go to other purchases, like paying down your credit cards from the wedding expenses you did incur, rather than dropping $20,000 on a newly remodeled kitchen.

Lifetime, WeTV, the Style Network—all of these lifestyle channels run contests and sweepstakes throughout the year, and even if you can't use the prize for your wedding, wouldn't it be a marvelous treat in the hectic months before your wedding to win an indulgent prize or a gift to give your parents?

Shopping may be part of your lifestyle, so subscribe to the Daily Candy newsletters in your region to possibly win some of their exciting prizes, like vacations, celebrity event swag bags, fashion items, cosmetics, makeovers, and freebies at some of their hand-picked hotspots. For the fashion minded, you won't want to miss out on the many sweepstakes that can hook you up with fabulous outfits and shoes for your prewedding parties, and your honeymoon, at such magazines and sites as *Allure, InStyle, Marie Claire,* and others.

Speaking of fashion, it's become a big Facebook and social media phenomenon for clothing stores to run major giveaways several times a year.

So be sure to "like" your favorite stores like Ann Taylor, White House Black Market, Forever 21, H & M, and others so that you know when they're running sweepstakes for a $250 or more shopping spree, which amounts to a free outfit for your rehearsal dinner, free clothes and accessories for your honeymoon, and just retail fabulousness in general.

PARENTS' MEDIA

You don't have to be a parent to click on the contest buttons to win cash for a new nursery, or a vacation, or baby gear to hang onto for "someday in the future." Check out *Parents, American Baby,* and Disney's *Family Fun* sites and social media outlets to possibly win a great prize or two.

LOCAL CONTESTS

On one balmy fall afternoon, I won $800 in a 50-50 drawing at a local high school football game. With $20 in tickets purchased to help support my husband's alma mater's football team, it was a good situation no matter if we won or not. But we did win. And $800 is not a small amount.

So consider fund-raising 50-50s to be part of your arsenal of potential freebies. It's not just high schools running them. It's churches, charities,

What to Expect

NOT ALL "JUNK" E-MAIL FROM CONTESTS ARE BAD

When you sign onto a clothing website's mailing list or newsletter, you're going to get weekly e-mails about sales and new arrivals. Consider the crowded inbox, ideally in a special e-mail account you've designated just for junk mail, an acceptable annoyance for what could turn into some excellent freebies. With a 40 percent off coupon, you could get free shoes to go with that dress—compared to what retail prices are. Besides coupons and sales, you'll also get member notifications about larger sweepstakes run by these companies.

and animal shelters, like the current 50-50 for my animal shelter for three $3 tickets—I wouldn't mind taking home its $25,000 prize. Not bad for a $9 investment.

Another staple of the local fund-raising scene is the Tricky Tray. That's the event where you buy a handful of tickets and deposit them into the bucket placed in front of a prize basket. I've seen tickets to NFL games, $500 gift cards to local restaurants that would make a fabulous setting for a free rehearsal dinner, beauty salon or spa packages that can be used for your free wedding morning hair, makeup, and nails. And other great items. So try your luck with those.

I wouldn't be a responsible journalist if I didn't warn you about the dangers of gambling. It's an addiction that can cost you a lot. So don't go overboard with buying lottery tickets, 50-50s, Tricky Tray tickets, and other chances to win anything. Set an acceptable amount of money for these fun events, and don't let yourself get bitten by the gambling bug. Because it has tremendous power to take over your life, ruin your marriage, wreck your credit, and wipe you out.

TELEVISION SHOW WEDDING CONTESTS

The odds of getting on a wedding reality show competition to win fabulous prizes are quite slim, but you never know. If your favorite television show or network announces that it's looking for real-life couples to compete for a free wedding or honeymoon, talk it over with your groom before you send in an application. You might not want to subject yourselves to some of the embarrassing contests that these shows involve. You don't want to be swimming through a mud pit in a wedding gown, or eating disgusting things, just to win a free wedding cake.

If you've seen a particular show and find that it doesn't require contestants to compromise their integrity or risk their professional and personal reputations, perhaps you'll choose to send in an entry.

Real Stories

TAP INTO THE TRICKY TRAY NETWORK

"The ladies in my mom's book club were a priceless source of information for which schools and charities run the best Tricky Trays. We were told which ones to go to, the ones with the most generous prizes, and which to skip. Mom and I attended one, and it was a blast. Turns out the local moms go to these as their big social hobby, bringing in their own catering for their table, and it's a raucous time as the lucky winners are called for their diamond bracelets, weekends at a vacation house, and roses made origami-style out of $20 bills."—Elizabeth, bride from New Jersey

Another angle of this category is the morning television talk show, such as *Today, Good Morning America,* and *Live with Kelly.* These shows don't aim to humiliate their contestants. They welcome videotaped entries of your story, with producers poring over thousands upon thousands of entries to choose their three or five finalist couples. They introduce the finalists to the world, share their tales, and America votes to give one couple the wedding of their dreams. America also gets to pick their dress, their cake, their bouquet, their rings, and just about everything else. You might be fine with giving up control of your wedding plans, for the chance to have a celebrity planner arrange your day, a fabulous designer gown and rings you'd never be able to afford, and the show's hosts as your wedding guests, plus a famous recording artist appearing on stage to sing your first dance song.

It can't hurt to enter these shows' calls for entries. You never know if you're exactly what they're looking for, and if the viewers will grant you the mega-valuable free wedding and honeymoon (also chosen by the viewers, in most cases). Again, check with your fiancé first, and decide if it would be your wedding dream come true to have *no* say in your wedding plans but get it all for free.

OTHER SOURCES OF SWEEPSTAKES

They're everywhere. I'm seeing many Etsy artists running giveaways of their creations, and restaurants are also posting sweepstakes for $250 gift cards or larger prizes on their Facebook pages. With social media running on the power of connection, companies of all types know that contests are a hot ticket for their exposure and that it's free for a company to post a giveaway on its Facebook page and let the news fly.

Worksheets

The worksheets here will help you keep fantastic control over all of your freebie-hunting strategies. If you've forgotten whom you asked for strings of lights, or how long it's been since the florist promised to send an amended contract with those free corsages for the moms, it's all right here, keeping you from getting frazzled and *sounding* frazzled when you ask friends, "I don't remember—did I ask you to lend me your strings of white lights for the terrace?" If you did ask, they'll chock it up to Overwhelmed Bride Syndrome. If you didn't ask, they'll assume you confused them with someone else.

Don't let the hectic pace of wedding planning, mixed with the legwork of freebie finding, get you into a stress spiral. Keep notes right here, and stay on top of it all.

Your Priority Lists

Which wedding elements are most important to you? The ones you're willing to spend the largest chunk of your budget on, to spare no expense, to get the best that's out there? The freebies you're getting make *these* categories doable when you have more money to devote to them.

For instance, most couples say their top wedding priority is the food. They want their guests to enjoy the most amazing gourmet cocktail party fare, with lots of stations, a gourmet sit-down dinner, and a delectable dessert bar and Belgian waffle station with homemade ice cream. *Menu* is their Priority No. 1.

Entertainment, too, is a top priority for most couples. They want a great band or DJ playing their favorite songs and interacting with their guests to keep the dance floor filled and the party going strong. The celebration hinges on having top-notch entertainers creating a mood, playing the perfect songs at the perfect times, and rocking it out to make their reception better than the hottest nightclub. That's Priority No. 2.

Other items that might be on your list of Top Five Priorities? Your gown, the flowers, your invitations, the cake.

Here, fill in your Top Five Priorities:

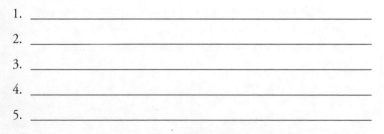

1. _____

2. _____

3. _____

4. _____

5. _____

Now, fill in your lesser priorities, the items you don't have your heart set on and are willing to arrange with a borrow or a barter, or accept as a free add-on from a vendor. They might be decor items, favors, Save-the-Dates, and more.

1. _____

2. _____

3. _____

4. _____

5. _____

Don't stop yourself at five. If you find additional items as you plan, jot them down here. And here's the fun part: If your parents or grandparents want to take on the planning of some wedding weekend element (and pay for it, making it free to you), this is the list of possibilities to scan.

If you don't have strong feelings about the location of the morning-after breakfast, then Mom and Dad get to run with the plans for it. It's the items you don't hold close to your heart that become a grab bag of opportunities for parents and others to enjoy planning, feel included, and add to the smash success of your wedding weekend. All free to you. So list some more ideas below:

6. _____

7. _____

8. _____

9. _____

10. _____

Networking and Contacts Lists

Keep your circle of generous lenders and vendors organized right here, with their contact information, so that you can check in, and—most importantly—say thank you.

Name	Address	Phone	E-mail	IM	Skype

Whom You've Asked for What

This might be your most often-used worksheet, as you look back to see whom you've contacted for a borrow, which vendors you've asked for add-ons, and who has told you they have freebies to give you.

Name	Offering

Requests Status Tracker

Keep track of which freebies are in the works, which have been delivered, and which you need to follow up on. With so many plans set in motion for every element of your day, this worksheet gets all of the freebie details out of your head and onto paper, making you more efficient and confident.

Name	Offering	When Asked	Follow-Up	Date Paid	Delivered

Name	Offering	When Asked	Follow-Up	Date Paid	Delivered

Bartering Worksheet

Brainstorm the types of products and services that you could get through bartering, using this worksheet:

Products:

1. _____

2. _____

3. _____

4. _____

5. _____

6. _____

7. _____

8. _____

9. _____

10. _____

Services:

1. _____

2. _____

3. _____

4. _____

5. _____

6. _____

7. _____

8. _____

9. _____

10. _____

Notes:

1. _____

2. _____

3. _____

4. _____

5. _____

6. _____

7. _____

8. _____

9. _____

10. _____

Budget Chart

Work your wedding budget right here, recording what you're paying for—
and getting that thrill when you're able to enter items in the FREE column.

Item/Service	Who's Paying	Budgeted Amount	Actual Amount	Date Paid	FREE
Engagement Announcement					
Engagement Portrait					
Engagement Party					
Wedding Website					
Wedding Coordinator					
Ceremony Venue					
Officiant's Fee					
Choir/Organist Fee					
Ceremony Decor					
Rentals for Ceremony					
Marriage License					
Reception Venue					
Reception Decor					
Reception Rentals					
Reception Site Preparations (Landscaping, etc.)					
Reception Staff (Valets, etc.)					

Item/Service	Who's Paying	Budgeted Amount	Actual Amount	Date Paid	FREE
Wedding Gown					
Fittings					
Veil & Headpiece					
Shoes					
Accessories					
Manicure					
Pedicure					
Facials					
Personal trainer					
Additional Beauty Treatments					
Wedding Day Hair					
Wedding Day Makeup					
Groom's Clothing					
Groom's Accessories					
Wedding Rings					
Save-the-Date Cards					
Invitations					
Wedding Programs					
Place Cards					
Menu Cards					
Additional Print Items					
Postage					

Item/Service	Who's Paying	Budgeted Amount	Actual Amount	Date Paid	FREE
Thank-You Notes					
Catering					
Wedding Cake					
Groom's Cake					
Additional Desserts					
Beverages					
Favors					
Flowers: Bouquets					
Flowers: Mothers' Flowers					
Flowers: Bridesmaid Bouquets					
Flowers: Boutonnieres					
Flowers: Centerpieces					
Flowers: Other					
Guest Book					
Gift Box or Display					
Photos or Frames					
Reception Entertainment					
Photography					
Videography					
Transportation					
Guest Transportation					
Rehearsal Dinner					

Item/Service	Who's Paying	Budgeted Amount	Actual Amount	Date Paid	FREE
Morning-After Breakfast					
Wedding Weekend Events					
Gifts for Each Other					
Gifts for Parents					
Gifts for Bridal Party					
Honeymoon					
Tips					
Gown Preservation					
Repairs & Replacements					
Additional Expenses:					

Resources

Note: This list is purely for your research and does not imply endorsement or recommendation of the companies or products. Since websites change over time, we apologize if any addresses have changed since the time of this printing.

WEDDING PLANNING WEBSITES

www.BridalGuide.com

www.Brides.com

www.DestinationIDoMag.com

www.GetMarried.com

http://Idoforbrides.com

www.MarthaStewart.com

www.MunaluchiBridal.com

http://SharonNaylor.net

www.SouthernBride.com

www.TheKnot.com

www.TownandCountryMag.com

www.WeddingChannel.com

DRESS TRADE

www.BridesmaidTrade.com

www.NewlyMaid.com

DEPARTMENT STORES AND CLOTHING STORES

www.AnnTaylor.com

www.Bloomingdales.com

www.Forever21.com

www.JCrew.com

www.Macys.com

www.Nordstrom.com

www.WhiteHouseBlackMarket.com

SHOES AND ACCESSORIES

www.AnnTaylor.com

www.BridalShoes.com

www.DavidsBridal.com

http://DiscountWeddingShoes.com

www.DSW.com

www.JCPenney.com

www.MyLittlePretty.com

www.ShoeBuy.com

www.Shoes.com

www.Zappos.com

BEAUTY

www.Avon.com

www.BobbiBrownCosmetics.com

www.CareFair.com

www.Clinique.com

www.ElizabethArden.com

RESOURCES

www.EsteeLauder.com

www.Lancome-USA.com

www.Loreal.com

www.MacCosmetics.com

www.MaxFactor.com

www.Maybelline.com

www.Neutrogena.com

www.Pantene.com

www.Revlon.com

www.Sephora.com

HAIRSTYLES

www.About.com

www.Beauty-and-the-Bath.com

http://DIY-Weddings.com

www.eHow.com

www.HairstyleZone.com

www.HerbalEssences.com

www.Suave.com

www.UpDoPrincess.com

www.YouTube.com

JEWELRY

www.AGS.org

www.Bluenile.com

www.DeBeers.com

Jewelry Information Center:
www.jig.org

www.Jewelry.com

www.Zales.com

INVITATIONS

http://AnnaGriffin.com

www.BotanicalPaperworks.com

www.Crane.com

www.Evite.com

www.Hallmark.com

www.Invitations4sale.com

www.InviteSite.com

http://MountainCow.com

www.PaperStyle.com

www.Papyrus.com

www.PSAEssentials.com

QUOTES AND POETRY

http://QuoteGarden.com

www.QuotesandSayings.org

http://QuotesPlanet.com

@TheLoveStories

MUSIC AND LYRICS

http://iTunes.com

www.LyricsDepot.com

www.LyricsFreak.com

www.Romantic-Lyrics.com

www.Spotify.com

LIMOUSINES

www.Limo.org

FLOWERS AND GREENERY

www.About.com

www.BHG.com

www.FloralDesignInstitute.com

www.HGTV.com

www.PAllenSmith.com

www.RomanticFlowers.com

www.SierraFlowerFinder.com

FOOD AND RECIPES

www.AllRecipes.com

www.BHG.com

www.FoodNetwork.com

WINE AND CHAMPAGNE

www.Wine.com

www.WineSpectator.com

RENTALS

www.Ararental.org

WAREHOUSE STORES

www.Bjs.com

www.Costco.com

www.SamsClub.com

CRAFTS AND PAPER

www.BHG.com

www.FlaxArt.com

www.HobbyLobby.com

www.LCIPaper.com

www.MarthaStewart.com

www.Michaels.com

www.OfficeMax.com

www.PaperDirect.com

www.Scrapjazz.com

www.Staples.com

TRAVEL

www.Amtrak.com

Bed and Breakfast Finder:
www.bnbfinder.com

Tourism Offices Worldwide Directory:
www.TOWD.com

SPECIAL EVENT ASSOCIATIONS

Association of Bridal Consultants:
www.bridalassn.com

International Special Events Society:
www.ises.com

Professional Photographers of America:
www.ppa.com

Wedding & Event Videographers
Association International:
www.weva.com

Wedding Officiants:
www.weddingofficiants.com

Wedding and Event Videographers
Association: www.weva.com

Wedding and Portrait Photographers
International: www.wppionline.com

WEATHER AND SUNSET

Sunrise and Sunset:
www.timeanddate.com

Sunrise Sunset Calendars:
www.sunrisesunset.com

www.WeatherChannel.com

PRICE COMPARISON SITES

www.BizRate.com

www.Dealtime.com

www.NextTag.com

www.PriceGrabber.com

www.Shopping.com

www.Shopzilla.com

@AboutFreebies

COUPON SOURCES

www.AllYou.com

www.CouponCabin.com

www.CouponDivas.com

www.CouponMom.com

www.Coupons.com

www.Groupon.com

www.LivingSocial.com

www.RetailMeNot.com

www.SwagGrabber.com

BARTERING SITES

www.Badabud.com

www.BarterQuest.com

www.Craigslist.org

www.Skills2Barter.com

www.SwagAGift.com

www.SwapStyle.com

www.SwapTree.com

www.ThingHeap.com

www.Trashbank.com

www.U-Exchange.com

BRIDALEXPOS

http://BridalShowcase.com

www.BridalShowExpo.com

http://Brideworld.com

www.ElegantBridalProductions.com

http://GreatBridalExpo.com

www.HereComestheGuide.com

www.TheBlingEvent.com

www.TheWeddingSalon.com

www.WeddingWire.com/bridalshows

CONTESTS AND SWEEPSTAKES

www.BHG.com

www.Brides.com

www.BridalGuide.com

www.BridalTweet.com

www.DIYNetwork.com

www.GetMarried.com

www.HGTV.com

www.LHJ.com

www.Parents.com

www.RealSimple.com

www.SwagGrabber.com

www.TheKnot.com

SEWING PATTERNS

http://AmyButlerDesign.com

www.BurdaStyle.com

www.Butterick.McCall.com

http://DIYFashion.About.com

www.FreeNeedle.com

www.M-Sewing.com

http://Sewing.About.com

www.Sewing.org

Additional Sites of Interest

www.CrateandBarrel.com: Free registering parties with appetizers and registry lessons

www.Hulu.com: Watch instructional videos for free, including crafts, dancing, workouts

http://iTunes.com: Use gift cards to load your own playlists for at-home or casual parties

http://Office.com/onotewedding: Free digital catchall for your wedding plans and images

www.WeddingMapper.com: Create your own wedding map, share the URL, and use its seating tool and budget tracker for free

www.WilliamsSonoma.com: Free cooking classes and registry events

Index

INDEX

About the Author

Sharon Naylor is the best-selling author of over thirty-five wedding books, contributing often to the top wedding magazines, websites, and blogs, including *Bridal Guide, Southern Bride, VOWS magazine, I Do For Brides, New Jersey Bride, Broke-Ass Bride,* Bride Tide, Wishpot, Best Wedding Sites, and many others. She has appeared as a wedding expert on *Good Morning America,* Martha Stewart Weddings Sirius Satellite Radio program, ABC News, *Get Married, I Do! with The Knot,* Lifetime, *Primetime, Inside Edition,* and many more.

Her books on bridal showers, etiquette, budget planning, personalizing your wedding, bridesmaid advice, and tips for the moms have all sat at the #1 spot on Amazon.com's best-sellers in wedding books and Kindle downloads.

Sharon's bridal articles have been syndicated by Huffington Post Weddings, Yahoo Shine!, Content That Works, and Creators Syndicate, and she is a member of eco-friendly site GorgeouslyGreen.com's 'Dream Team' as their green weddings expert.

She has also been featured in *InStyle Weddings, Modern Bride, Glamour, Marie Claire, Self, Shape, Redbook, The Wall Street Journal, The New York Times, TheStreet.com, Bankrate.com,* among many other top media outlets.

She is the Wedding Spokesperson for the iconic New York City chocolatier Li-Lac Chocolates, and blogs as the honeymoon and destination wedding spokesperson for Caneel Bay and Jumba Bay, both Rosewood Resorts, and has appeared as a top celebrity wedding expert at elite bridal industry events such as the Conde Nast Dream House, The Wedding Salon, and other star-studded bridal programs.

She lives in Morristown, New Jersey with her husband Joe.